Your Free Resources

Don't forget your free resources that go along with this book!

You can access them right now to start taking action towards your dream career.

The free resources include:

- An online masterclass on agile leadership
- A compilation of my favorite journal prompts to start journaling today
- A downloadable guide with five easy steps to better financial health
- A subscription to my newsletter with leadership/career tips and strategies in your inbox

Get access here:

www.nadahmed.com/resources

Dedication

This book is dedicated to all the ambitious women out there. I want each and every one of you to have the career of your dreams and to know that it is possible—despite how stuck you may be feeling right now.

Table of Contents

Foreword

"Manage your energy," my then boss said.

Meh. It wasn't the advice I wanted to hear. I was twenty-two and struggling in my dream job. At the time, I was single and had plenty of space in my life to build a career. I worked eighteen-hour days sometimes to make my boss happy. For months, I couldn't comprehend why my dedication and rigorous work ethic weren't appreciated. I would bang my head against the wall and poke at my self-worth, asking questions like "Am I qualified?" and "Why can't I do this?"

What I learned with time (and many more jobs) as I progressed the ladder was that I rubbed people the wrong way with my enthusiasm and energy for work and life. It was a lesson that took me nearly twenty years to learn, but I finally embraced a new paradigm: I didn't need to change myself to fit in, but rather, I needed to design and create a life and career that would embrace my energy so that I would stand out. The world needs good troublemakers—that's how we move wo(man)kind forward.

I also took up running. Because I have the energy to lead "unwanted projects" and do "hairy audacious things" and I'm a "force of nature" (words all given in past performance reviews by bosses and by my parents), I have learned I need outlets to channel my energy.

I also learned I need to find the right "crew" and create a village of people around me who hold a similar mindset. Don't get me wrong, I am the CEO of a company that focuses on increasing diversity, so difference matters to me. But when you're a woman on fire with things to do in this life, you must keep company that can appreciate your zest and will encourage you to keep leading. What you consume and who you interact with, along with vision, will, and grit, are what create a successful network.

I felt a bit lonely at times in my career. Sometimes I still do. It's not easy leading change. The way I started to create a support system to help me was by finding people I admired and following their work. And I didn't go small either. I began admiring presidents, heads of state, and others at a very early age. I'm a woman who believes you must surround yourself with greatness—including both women and men.

One of my mentors, Sheryl Sandberg, former COO of Meta and Facebook, wrote *Lean In*. Her words "What would you do if you weren't afraid?" resonated with me. Let's face it: we all have fears. After hitting the wall a few times in my careers, always learning, my fear wasn't failing again, but rather succeeding. After meeting Sheryl, I was inspired to start my own company and chart a career very different from the one I started. Most recently, I also began to follow Ray Dalio, the billionaire entrepreneur who started Bridgewater Associates from his bedroom decades ago. His book *Principles for Dealing with the Changing World Order* is a 500-page bible that identifies metrics from our history that can be applied to understand today's changing world.

This book, *Determined to Lead*, is an invaluable resource to the game changers, misfits, and audacious forces of nature (yes, you) who need the reminder that the world needs us. We live in challenging times, divided with big needs. The world's demand for energy is rising, economic gaps are widening between the haves and the have-nots, and our climate needs changing. The system isn't working for many, and that's why it needs something different. This system was built by men post-World War II with an economic boom that has afforded the last two generations tremendous wealth. But it's excluded the other half of our world and intellectual power: women. So, I argue that the new world order doesn't just need historical data and principles by which we lead; it needs to harness the power of the feminists and allies in all of us. It's our time to rise, take a seat at the table, and pave a new future for generations to come.

When author and colleague Nada Ahmed asked me to write the foreword to her masterpiece, I was honored. This book is a no-nonsense, no-BS approach to how to bet and invest in the best stock you own: *you*. Nada and I want and *need* you to join us on this journey with many others who are changing the system, redefining the rules, and giving our kids the future they deserve.

Katie Mehnert, CEO and founder, ALLY Energy (she/her)

A modern architect of the energy workforce, Katie Mehnert is the founder and CEO of ALLY Energy, the community accelerating connections, jobs, and skills to drive an equitable energy transition. ALLY Energy is an inaugural member of Greentown Labs Houston, the top climate tech incubator in North America.

Mrs. Mehnert has held global leadership roles with BP and Shell in safety and environment during periods of financial crisis, spills, divestment, and globalization. Her early career included assignments with Duke Energy, Entergy, and Enron. Her corporate path drove her to entrepreneurship to help energy companies prepare for the looming talent shortage and meet the workforce diversity needs necessary to address energy poverty and climate change.

She was appointed ambassador to the United States Department of Energy in 2020 during the Trump administration and has testified before Congress on the clean energy workforce of the future. She was also appointed by the Biden administration to the National Petroleum Council. She's also an Energy Institute Fellow and an advisor to Clean Energy for America.

Mrs. Mehnert is a speaker, author, and trusted source in the energy industry. She has been published in *Scientific American, Forbes, The Hill, CNBC, and CNN.* Her first book, *Grow with the Flow,* was published in 2020. She most recently coauthored *Everyday Superheroes: Women in Energy,* a children's book focused on energy careers. Mrs. Mehnert also has appeared in *Hot Money,* a documentary starring Award-winning actor Jeff Bridges and retired NATO General Wesley Clark on the financial complexities of climate change and finance.

Mrs. Mehnert is a four-time World Major marathoner, having completed London, Chicago, New York, and Berlin. Her husband is vice president of legal with Baker Hughes. They live with their twelve-year-old daughter, Ally, in Houston.

Author's Note

One day, my husband asked me what I would write about if I could write a book today. I knew the answer right away: agile leadership, which has been the focus of my work for the past decade, specifically how to lead multidisciplinary, diverse innovation teams rooted in the principles of agile from software development. I am obsessed with what it takes to be an effective leader and what kind of leadership is needed in the postindustrial era, and I am frequently asked to speak on the topic. It was obvious that it was a topic that I deeply understand and can help people with.

The seed was planted, and I could not shake off the idea of a book.

This was August 2020, smack in the middle of a roaring pandemic. I was just about to go back to work after six months of maternity leave. I had been promoted to VP of transformation at one of the leading engineering and technology companies in Norway. *Wow*, I thought, *I will be in a great position to document tangible stories from real-life leadership experience for my book.*

It goes without saying that 2020 was a year of unprecedented events.

The pandemic threw a wrench in all my plans. I adjusted and made new plans, only to see them, too, decimated by the wrath of the pandemic. In the midst of it all, it seemed like the only thing I could reasonably plan for was the unexpected.

From 2020 to 2021, as I took on a new leadership role, I was tested as a leader on many levels. I kept a notebook with me where I recorded my reflections and stories that would be perfect for this book. Toward the end of 2021, though, it became apparent that the book will take a slightly different turn.

What This Book Is Really About

My career has been built on forming and coaching teams developing innovative business solutions through new products and services. I have extensively studied what makes the perfect innovative environment, how to brainstorm ideas, and how to get teams to think outside the box and put aside their own biases and limiting beliefs. One of the fundamental mistakes teams make is that they jump too quickly to solutions. In a world where we value action and urgency, there is immense pressure to see quick results. I want to see quick results too. But I teach teams to linger on the questions. Are we addressing the right question? Ask the wrong question and you end up solving the wrong problem, creating a solution no one needs.

I kept on falling into the solution trap as I was writing this book. Most of the guides available for writing nonfiction books guide us toward a generic how-to framework. According to one book coach, readers choose to buy books for one of two reasons: to be entertained or to solve a problem.

I am not a fiction writer (yet), so my focus had to be a problem I was solving.

Could it be that I . . .

. . . help leaders become more agile, empathetic, and inclusive so that they can lead teams that thrive in the rapidly changing digital age?

That wasn't quite hitting the spot.

But I charged ahead, speed over quality. I picked a book thesis and moved forward. A few days in, I was listening to an episode of Brené Brown's podcast in which she interviewed James Clear, the author of *Atomic Habits*. He talked about a conversation he had had with his publisher in which he had laid out his frustrations with the writing process, particularly how ironic he found it that writing a book on habits seemed to be wrecking his own personal habits. He laughed.

This is when his publisher said something deeply profound that changed everything for him (and for me): "We write the books we need."[1]

I was in the middle of emptying the dishwasher when I heard this, and my entire being screeched to a halt. I hit rewind.

We write the books that *we* need.

Instead of thinking about this book as a product that sells, perhaps I could think of it as the book that I would have needed on my career journey.

What would I write for someone like me? Someone with all of the same dreams and aspirations for her career that I had had for mine? What kind of book would have helped me to be better prepared for the highs and, particularly, the lows?

What kind of book did I need that did not exist yet?

That is how I discovered my audience. It's me. It's people like me. That disruptive woman full of ambition who does not always follow the rules, who charts her own path, who speaks up, who does not let other people's limiting beliefs define her. A woman who is determined to lead.

---

1   Brené Brown, interview with James Clear, "Brené with James Clear on Atomic Habits, Part 1 of 2," November 15, 2021, in Dare to Lead with Brené Brown, podcast, MP3 audio, 49:51, *https://brenebrown.com/podcast/atomic-habits-part-1-of-2/*.

Being different and staying different is hard work, and I wish there was a book that was written for people like us, people who are disruptive. Through their courage and rebellion, they are the driving force of positive change in the workplace today. And they need a voice. This book is that voice.

Chapter 1:

Where One Story Ends, Another Begins

So often in life, things that you regard as an impediment turn out to be great, good fortune.

— Ruth Bader Ginsburg

It was time for a quarterly one-on-one with Mario, my boss.

As I entered the virtual room, I was surprised to see that a representative from HR was there as well. The HR representative informed me that she had invited my boss's boss, Erik, who had hired me for my role six months prior. I immediately registered that this was not a regular meeting.

The meeting started with an onslaught of questions: How do you think you are doing? Do you think you are able to manage this role? Is this too much for you? Perhaps we need a different setup?

I was not prepared for this. I started to defend myself, overwhelmed by all the questions being thrown at me. They wanted to convey a message, but I couldn't quite hear it. I was speaking, but my words made no sense, and soon enough I was cut off. I felt words being put into my mouth; they were pushing me into saying that my position wasn't working, that I could not manage this job, that it was too much for me.

My mind was racing. I was processing what was being said while desperately trying to figure out the best response to save the situation. *What do they want me to say? Do I want to say what they want me to say? Abort. Please abort!*

Finally, it came, what I had been fearing all along. They threw an option on the table, a proposal. The chatter in my head stopped. My brain was yanked back into the present moment, on full alert. A thick patch of incertitude suddenly lifted and I could see clearly again. I registered what was going on: they wanted to take away my dream job. I knew exactly what I had to do.

I stopped playing defense. I clearly stated what I wanted: I wanted to keep my role and my team. I agreed that the current setup was not perfect and that perhaps I should be reporting to someone other than Mario. I reiterated the importance of keeping my team, which I had carefully hired and was continuing to build, stressing with all my heart and soul how important my team was to me. I shared our goals, our vision, and how we would get there. I could save this!

The call went silent.

Finally, Mario spoke. "Nada, I gave you my feedback a few weeks ago. I told you what is not working. Now either you need to change, or we will need to make some changes."

The call ended.

I was left sitting in front of my screen, staring at my crammed calendar. What did he mean? Was the feedback he had given me a few weeks before a warning? *I haven't even been in this role for six months! I am just getting started. This is my dream job. It cannot just end here,* I thought.

I replayed the conversation in my head several time before I called Erik. Erik was not only Mario's boss, but he was also my mentor and my biggest supporter in this new role.

"What was this interrogation all about? What is going on?" I asked desperately.

Erik responded calmly. "That was just a conversation. We wanted to get your view on how you think you are doing. And we are just testing a few potential changes. Anyway, Nada, you should really consider whether you want this role. It's not a nine-to-five job, and you are a mother with young kids."

His last comment threw me off. I was seriously confused.

Being a mom has nothing to do with this. Why is he bringing that up? I could feel the feminist in me being provoked. I took a deep breath to rein her in. Don't get hung up on his comment.

He does not get you. You have never once considered that having kids, being a mom, would get in the way of your career. Never. He does not understand that these days, being a mom is irrelevant to a woman's career journey.

I shrugged off the motherhood comment and continued making my case. I desperately wanted to hear him say, "Nada, I've got your back. You are valuable to this company. You deserve to be here."

Instead, all I could hear was *Nada, you can't do this job. It is too much work. You are a mother. You do not have it in you. You cannot handle this. It requires more than you are able to give right now.*

I hung up. It began to dawn on me: the inevitability of what was to come.

A few weeks later, I got a call from HR, letting me know that they were making a "small" change. My boss was going to take over my team, and I would have a new role. My team, which I had so thoughtfully crafted. I had handpicked each one of them and earnestly persuaded them to join me on this incredible journey. I had been so excited to be the best leader I could be for them.

I had failed. I had let them down.

I sank into the feeling of loss. Everything I had invested in, everything I had built, all that defined me, was gone. My dream eviscerated, my relationships severed, and all my investment of time, energy, and emotions gone to waste.

Just a few months before, I had been floating in the clouds, overjoyed to have the role of a lifetime. I had been proud, so proud, that I had finally made it! I had thought that my career was finally on track. I had had everything I ever wanted, everything that I had been chasing for years. I had had a wonderful team that I was so grateful for. I had been living my dream.

As I write this, I am coming out of a year in which I experienced the biggest loss of my career. I had been at the pinnacle of my leadership journey, and the rug had been pulled out from under my feet. My shadow had fallen flat on her face, while I, like the kid from *The Karate Kid*, jumped high in the air and assumed my most fierce position before I landed firmly back on the ground, ready for combat.

Why would I start my book, which is meant to be about empowering other women to rise to the top, with this story of a time I faced a huge setback? Because I want this book to be grounded in reality. I want to use this book to not only guide you through creating an amazing career for yourself, but also to raise important issues that women and those of us who are different face. I do not want to gloss over the challenges, the pain, and the emotional turmoil of being an ambitious woman who goes against the grain. I want to encourage you to be you, but also to know that struggle and constant work await you on this journey. It is an entire package of joy and also some amount of pain that makes it all worth it. The challenges and the pain make us into the person who is capable of surmounting any hurdles along our path and who appreciates the accomplishments fully and wholeheartedly.

Through this book, I want to help other women leaders better understand the challenges we are up against when we decide to lead in a different way. I want to equip you with the right tools and strategies so that you are prepared for the journey and can start designing your own unique path to a successful career. There will be setbacks, and, as bruised as you may be, I want to inspire you to get back up again.

Throughout my career, powerful, successful women and men have told me again and again to not focus on the difference, to just smile and fit in. *Do what they do and you will be fine. Brush off the issues, the biases, and the prejudice. We are bigger than that, and the only way to overcome is to show that we can fit in, that we can play the game too. Lean in and you will be fine. Most of all, do not complain.*

The truth is that we are not fine. I was not fine. Women are leaving corporate at an increasing pace all across the board. There is not just one broken rung, but many broken rungs. In particular, the rung where we rise to middle management and start having a voice. That is when we are tested the most on our willingness to compromise to remain within the system and continue striving to reach for the higher echelons of corporate.

I am writing the book that I needed to read.

I would have loved to read a book by someone who had gone through their career journey being different, someone who was now recounting the struggles they faced driving change and hitting against a wall again and again. Someone who was hired because they were different but ended up feeling like they didn't really belong, like their difference was not really valued.

What did they do, how did they feel and react? How did they prevail?

This book will not give you all the solutions. It won't give you the formula to have that LinkedIn-perfect career. There is no formula, and there is no such thing as a perfect career. Instead, I want to share what I did, what worked for me and what did not, how I failed, and what mistakes I made.

This book is not a practical how-to guide. There is no single "how-to." Life does not come with a manual. You have to do the hard work to find out what works for you. This book does, however, contain a compilation of my best tips, which I hope will inspire you and provide you with some guidance on your journey.

I hope this book will raise more questions in your mind than it will answer. I hope that the questions that come up for you will help you reach the state of awakening earlier than I did so that instead of building your *CV*, you can start building your *career* from a place of love, joy, and freedom.

My purpose as a leader is to guide people toward a deeper understanding of the problem they are trying to solve. I ensure that we invest time in exploring the right questions before we start fixing a given problem. Investing in sustainable solutions means doing the hard work of understanding what is not working at the moment. That is what this book is about: investigating the real issues that are not only holding back women but stifling creativity, innovation, and transformation so that we can start devising solutions appropriate to our needs and making real business impact.

This Is Not a Regular Self-Help Book

Most self-help books assume that everyone is the same. They say, "If you follow what I did, the way I did it, you will become rich and successful and achieve whatever your goal is." What they ignore is that everyone is different. What works for you may not work for me. You might have gotten lucky on your journey, and I may get completely unlucky on my own.

While luck does have something to do with your career journey, I believe you can increase your chances of getting lucky by putting yourself out there and getting really good at what you do. As you get skilled, it becomes harder and harder to distinguish when your progress is a matter of luck or hard work.

In this book, I take you through my journey and the lessons I am taking with me to the next phase of my career. I hope this will inspire those who can relate to the struggles and dreams that I have had. I want to let you know that you are not alone in your struggles. The most successful and inspiring people have been where you are today and have felt like you are feeling, and if you are feeling stuck, there are ways of getting unstuck. You deserve to be here. There is nothing wrong with you. The parts about you that are rough on the edges, that make others uncomfortable, are your biggest asset.

In the next chapters, I will take you through my journey of agile leadership. I will cover what it is like to be a woman in masculine structures and share the struggles, the trials, the tribulations, and all the ways in which I have empowered myself. By following my lead, you, too, will be able to empower yourself—with fewer challenges along the way.

I hope you come away from this book with tangible ideas for how you can level up in your career, get unstuck, and take some big leaps without compromising who you are. We are all in this together . . . and we will get through this together.

Chapter 2:

From Rebel to Leader:
How Did We Get Here?

I am not what I think I am; I am not what you think I am.
I am what I think you think I am.

— *Charles Horton Cooley*

My Rebellious Beginning

During my childhood in Pakistan, my parents were very deliberate about ensuring that both my sister and I grew up as empowered, independent women. They didn't limit us to stereotypical roles, and they made us believe that we could succeed in any profession we wanted. My mom promised that she would have the same rules for us that she did for our brother. But as I grew older, we all realized that that was not possible in the society we lived in. Suddenly, after I became a teenager, there were rules imposed on me: what I could do, where I could go, and what I should wear. Like every teenager, I rebelled. I could not stand having to abide by rules that seemed so unfair for girls. I remember opening my journal one day and writing, "I hate being a girl. I wish I was a boy." My journal was filled with stories of despair, anguish, injustice, and false promises—but it was also filled with dreams and hopes of a future where freedom has no bounds.

I was determined to leave Pakistan as soon as I could. I longed to explore the world outside, where society did not impose rules on me regarding what I should wear or if I could ride my bike to visit my friend. I wanted to go somewhere where I did not feel that all eyes were on me at all times, judging my every move.

Every single day from when I was thirteen till the day I left Pakistan at sixteen, I planned my escape. I channeled my anger and frustration into my schoolwork. It was my way out. I explored all my options and planned meticulously so that I could get a scholarship to study abroad. I studied diligently, amassed a portfolio of accomplishments, and applied everywhere.

One day, it happened. I got a call. One of the schools that I had applied to had a spot for me! Unbelievable. Even to this day, I get goosebumps thinking about it. Out of the thousands of applicants, they had chosen me; luck had met preparedness. I received a United World College (UWC) scholarship to go study at Li Po Chun United World College of Hong Kong for my last two years of high school. That scholarship changed everything for me.

I remember arriving at the Hong Kong airport with one big suitcase and being struck by the beautiful architecture around me. The airport had a majestic feel. It was clean, shiny, and spacious. I was in the New York City of Asia. I was picked up by students one year senior to me, and they guided me to the red double-decker bus that stopped closest to our school. I sat upstairs at the front of the bus, simply mesmerized by the breathtaking views of Hong Kong Island, the ocean, the mountains, and the skyscrapers. I pinched myself to confirm that my dream had come true.

UWC further nurtured my rebellious spirit. It was a boarding school whose students were high achievers from all around the world, all of us passionate and determined to change the world and make it a better place for everyone. Everything we did was purpose-driven, and being around people who were so vastly different from us continuously inspired us to learn from each other, have difficult conversations, and grow as human beings. We were taught to take responsibility and were encouraged to fight for what we believed in. My time at UWC made me believe that I was at this school because I was going to change the world. I was going to champion all kinds of causes that would make the world a more peaceful, just, and equitable place. I was being educated and primed to fight for causes bigger than myself. There was so much that needed to change. Through my life experiences, through all that I had been told, through all that I had read, I was being conditioned to be a disruptor, to be the driver of change.

Determined to Lead

For as long as I can remember, I have always wanted to lead. I love inspiring and motivating others. I love taking charge and guiding and helping others to achieve their goals. You cannot be a leader if you are not helping others, but I also know I can't personally be a great leader unless I really want to be, unless I find leading deeply satisfying and am willing to take risks and be that trailblazer into uncharted territory.

My time as the president of the International Club at my college in the US was one of my earliest adult leadership roles. I was striving to drive change in a divided college environment where the international students did not effectively mingle with the local Americans. I was motivated by what diversity had to offer. I wanted everyone to experience the richness of cross-cultural exchanges and the depth of what we could learn from those different from us, just as I had at UWC.

Once I entered the workplace, I created more opportunities to practice leadership, both at work and outside of it. I launched a nonprofit organization, TCF Norway, consisting of a small team and twenty-plus volunteers, where we collected funds to successfully build and sustain a school in Pakistan. I wanted other girls from Pakistan to experience the same freedom I had had as a result of a high-quality education. My work with TCF Norway not only allows me to give back, but it also allows me to practice leadership in an environment where everyone is volunteering their time. Since launching, I have of course made plenty of mistakes and experienced my share of setbacks. How do you motivate people and hold them accountable when you are not paying their salaries? Well, it turns out that that is what true leadership is about: creating influence and motivating people toward action, even without official authority.

I noticed the leaders who motivated and inspired me, leaders who believed in me and showed it by giving me challenging tasks. They gave me autonomy to be creative and work in my own way. These were leaders who let me make mistakes so that I could take even bigger risks and stretch a little bit more each time. So I began to mimic their behavior, and I began to talk about how I wanted to lead. My passion for leadership began to show, and eventually people began to reach out and ask me to talk to their organizations and their teams about leadership, particularly agile leadership, which I will explain in more detail later.

Conforming and the Nonconforming Me

We all try to fit into the societies we live in. As the sociologist Charles Horton Cooley said, "I am what I think you think I am." As much as we try to be unique, we not only mirror those around us but we try to be what others expect us to be. I am on a journey now where I am trying to free myself of such expectations so that I can live life fully.

When I was younger and had recently started my first job, I did not know what it meant to be myself. I did not know myself enough to feel confident. I looked at those around me who held roles I wanted to hold one day, and I tried to be like them. Watching them taught me how to run meetings, execute projects, and make complex spreadsheets. I experimented a lot. To begin with, I worked on honing everything. With time, I focused on what gave me more joy and satisfaction, what came easier to me than to others. When I learned more about myself, it became easier for me to express myself as my own person.

The success I have had in corporate, though, usually came when I ventured off the beaten path and tried something different. I used my creativity, and it brought me immense happiness, joy, and fulfillment, and, as a result, my career took off.

My first big jump of responsibility came when I was asked to lead an innovation program on big data and automation. This was a completely new area for me—and for the company. I could afford the freedom to be creative and try different things. Luckily, I had a boss who embraced my creative and adventurous spirit. He encouraged me and believed in me more than I believed in myself. I enrolled in different meetups in the city that focused on big data and tried to learn as much as I could. This brought me into connection with the startup world, and I learned about agile, lean startup, and design thinking. Building new products, understanding the customers and their pain points, and developing go-to-market strategies is where I was bringing in my strength and my true creative self.

Experiencing Turbulence

My career was not a continuous upward trajectory. Careers often aren't, yet we expect them to be. We may think that many of those we admire are experiencing continuous positive progress, but when you dig deeper, you will see that we all have our own detours into valleys of immense growth accompanied by struggle. We do not see the pain that comes with the journey, as people mostly share their highs on social media. Sharing when you are not at your best, when you encounter a setback, is uncomfortable. Being vulnerable is hard work, and many of us do not know how and why we need to be vulnerable. The biggest leadership lesson that the universe keeps throwing at me is that I can't be authentic without being vulnerable.

I have spent my entire career working on building myself to be the best leader that I could be. Over the past ten years, I have developed my own leadership philosophy inspired by agile principles. I have been asked to speak on this topic on multiple platforms around the world.

Yet, when I finally embodied that leader, I was thrown a curveball. I was in what I thought was my dream job for less than six months before I was removed from my role and asked to take on another one. It was a big blow to my ego. The coup de grâce that spewed me out of the system. I had reached the pinnacle of my leadership journey, seen my dream come true, gotten a taste, and then, just like that, had it callously taken away.

I felt shame as part of me took this decision as a verdict on my performance. In reality, it may have had nothing to do with my performance. All I was told about the decision was that it was part of "restructuring" to create a more efficient organization. Why, then, was I taking it so personally?

Simply because I had attached myself—and my self-worth—too tightly to the role, to the title. I debated over and over what I could have done differently, concluding that there was no way that I could have guaranteed a different outcome. I could have done everything in my power to keep the role and still lost it regardless.

As I process the pain, I learn that, even after this setback, I am still the same winner that I was before. I am the same person, and my experience, my competence, and my skills cannot be taken away, even though my title was. I am still the same champion who climbed the ladder; I was never an impostor.

Once I started believing that I am not an impostor, I began to let go of the shame. Once I started letting go of shame, I could forgive myself and others and start moving on with grace.

Letting go of shame allowed me to see who I had become. This person chasing a title at the cost of everything else was not me. That person was being transformed to the new me, who realized that I did not need a title. I could assign myself whatever title I wanted. I had proven myself.

I share this story now, before I dive into all my leadership lessons, in order to let you know that I am far from perfect and that my own amazing career has had its pitfalls. Yet, even in face of such setbacks, I am able to stand strong on the foundation I have built over the past two decades. I will not let setbacks stand in my way and chip away at my own belief in myself.

It is when no one else believes in you that you need that stellar belief in yourself. You have to be your own cheerleader. And when you do that, you will find that your own belief is enough to propel you forward.

Disrupting Myself

The realization that I have proven myself, that I have arrived at my destination that I had set out for myself a decade ago, made me reframe losing my dream job as an inflection point, an opportunity to think bigger about my goals, my ambitions, and my next destination. I did well for myself, for a girl from Islamabad. Today, I am a woman with rich living and working experiences spanning five countries across the globe. I have amassed immense knowledge, expertise, and wisdom in various industries. I overcame challenges that seemed insurmountable and reached goals that seemed preposterous. I prevailed with pure determination. I am no longer just a girl from Islamabad, trying to prove myself.

Today, I have more faith in myself and my own capabilities than ever before. It turned out that my career disruption came at a perfect time for me to step out of corporate to make a bigger impact, to start my own business. In the past year, I have launched my company, Agile Leadership, where I help businesses with innovation and growth strategies. I have launched two podcasts, *Braving Innovation*, where I hold conversations with global leaders and share inspiring stories, tips, and strategies to help others on their journeys as innovation leaders, entrepreneurs, and investors, and *Women Writing Checks*, a podcast for women in venture capital. I speak on global stages on topics I feel passionate about. I am an angel investor in companies that are solving pressing problems for society. I am in boardrooms of companies at the cutting edge of innovation and technology, working to ensure that these businesses have a positive impact on society and the environment. I am excited about endless opportunities and the great adventures that lie ahead. I have the wisdom that I have gained over the past decade to know that a career is not always a linear, smooth upward trajectory. The joy is in embracing every curve and trough as much as the peaks, for within the challenges lie important lessons and guidance for the journey. The joy is in knowing that you can trust yourself to handle whatever life throws at you and make the best of it.

So let's begin!

Chapter 3:

Agile Leadership:
What Leadership Means to Me

Who we are is how we lead.

— *Brené Brown*

We Are All Leaders

Leadership is not a title given to you; it is assumed. Almost all of us assume leadership in some aspect of our lives, whether at work or elsewhere. Plenty of people who are in positions of power and authority do not display leadership, while others who have no title connected to them amass substantial power and influence. Take Greta Thunberg and Malala Yousafzai. Both are young women without official titles or authority, but they have managed to mobilize millions of people to drive change for causes they feel passionately about. On the other hand, I have encountered managers who have authority but lack influence. They use authority to make their teams do things they do not want to do, but authority alone will not inspire people to go above and beyond. Leadership is when you can inspire people to do what they never thought they were capable of doing.

Everyone can choose to practice leadership. We assume leadership when we make a tough call, when we mentor a young colleague, when we invite a new teammate to lunch, when we challenge executive management, or when we stand by a decision. We assume leadership when we generate a following and our colleagues look up to us, seek our expertise, thought leadership, and advice.

Leaders come in all forms. Some leaders are inspirational and visionary, others bring structure and reason during times of chaos, and some manage to do both. I use the term *agile leadership* to embody all types of leadership as long as they are rooted in agile values of human-centricity, value-adding work, collaboration, and resilience. I want to make sure that we capture the diversity of leadership that exists and acknowledge that there is no one way to be a leader and that we require different types of leadership depending on the goals we are trying to achieve.

In this chapter, I share with you how you can start showing up as a leader today and use agile values to influence your teams and those around you and amplify your impact. The principles and values that I discuss in this chapter have allowed me to be who I am while empowering those around me to be better versions of themselves.

What is agile leadership?

In the late '90s, developers were struggling to cope with the increased complexity of software development. Projects were taking years to complete and were ending up delayed and massively over budget. Often, by the time projects had been completed, the software technology was outdated, or customer demands had changed, resulting in suboptimum solutions. The traditional approach was not working.

Developers started experimenting with a new way of working that allowed them to deal with the uncertainties of the real world. They realized that the measures of control inherent in the traditional project management system made that system less capable of adapting to the rapidly changing environment. They began working in a way that would later be called agile, a mindset in which, instead of strict control, users take advantage of the changing system, experiment, and adapt quickly. This new approach was an iterative and fluid form of management where progression was not in one linear direction. Instead, teams worked concurrently and maintained a continuous feedback loop, allowing for quick changes. This led to a more efficient way of working. It enabled teams to develop products more quickly and better cater to customer needs.

At its core, agile methodology is about handing more power to the people. It pushes a larger proportion of decision-making to employees on the front lines, who are frankly best suited to make those decisions. It's built on the Toyota Andon Cord concept, that any employee can disrupt the flow of production if they see a defect. Agile is about creating a culture where each employee is empowered to make decisions. Employees don't wait for permission from their supervisors. They pull the cord—because they have been trusted to make decisions and assume responsibility. As a leader, your ultimate goal is to get work done through and with people, and agile gives you the foundation to do just that.

"The Agile Manifesto" was written in 2001 and proposed these four values:

1. Individuals and interactions over processes and tools.
2. Working software over comprehensive documentation.
3. Customer collaboration over contract negotiation.
4. Responding to change over following a plan.[2]

These values were specific to software development, but in this postindustrial era, non-development teams are also adopting the agile mindset. Whether we are working on software or leading teams in other areas, these agile values are extremely valuable in this highly complex and rapidly changing world.

Drawing from my experience building agile teams in big and complex organizations for the past decade, I translate these

---

2   Mike Beedle et al. "*Manifesto for Agile Software Development," accessed January 23, 2023,* https://agilemanifesto.org/.

foundational agile values and principles into leadership. An agile leader will let go of control to give people room to adapt more rapidly, to make mistakes and learn from them, and to take on more accountability.

Agile Values

Original Agile Manifesto	Individuals and interactions over processes and tools	Working software over comprehensive documentation	Customer collaboration over contract negotiation	Responding to change over following a plan
Agile Leadership	**Human-Centricity**	**Value-adding work**	**Collaboration**	**Resilience**

Figure 1: Agile Values (Illustration by author).

Let's take a deep dive into each one of these four values and how they all translate to leadership.

1. Human-Centricity (Individuals and Interactions over Processes and Tools)

Agile leadership is about focusing on the people at the core of solving problems and achieving goals. How we achieve our goals is important, but not as important as the outcome itself. One of the fundamental mistakes we make is giving more power to the process, so much so that we are not willing to make exceptions even when we know that doing so will be good for business (and society). Instead, we stick to the process and lock ourselves into suboptimal decisions, even when new data emerges that suggests that a different approach might be more effective.

Agile mindset ensures that processes and tools do not get in the way of achieving our goals. Instead, an agile mindset allows us to create a culture where the human brain is empowered to think and devise new systems catered toward our needs. The team is at the center, and tools and processes support them; however, the people are prioritized over the processes and the tools. An agile mindset keeps a constant focus on the people and their well-being to ensure psychological safety for a high-performance culture.

Processes and tools are obviously important, but they come second to people. We have to trust people first and give them the ability to deviate from the process to produce better results.

A few years ago, the company I worked for did a major reorganization, and all leadership teams were dissolved to form new ones. Once the executive leadership team was announced, we had two weeks to select the leaders below them (L3), then another two weeks for the leaders below that (L4). I was charged with forming two strategic teams, which we needed to put in place urgently, and was given the permission to hire right away and not wait until the other L3s and L4s were in place.

I reached out to candidates and, if they were interested, I made them offers. When one of the candidates' managers found out that I had approached him with an offer outside of the agreed-upon process, the manager called me fuming, telling me that I had deviated from the process and that that was not acceptable. I explained the situation and the reason for the exception. However, for this manager, a deviation from the process, even with the right permissions, was a grave offense. He decided to do everything in his power so that his employee could not accept my offer. I didn't have a chance to compete with the manager's aggressive campaign to prevent this employee from taking my offer. Eventually, the employee was fed up and left the company. Process won and, as a result, we lost a talented employee.

If, in my example, we had been operating in an agile environment, the manager would have consulted the employee and understood that this role aligned with his ambitions and, even if I had not followed the process, the manager would have prioritized what was best for the person and the business. Instead, he chose to stick to his principle of adhering to the process, and he punished anybody who did not, regardless of the outcome. I deviated from the process, but only because the process was getting in the way of achieving our ultimate goal, which was to form this team before the deadline.

2. Value-Adding Work (Working Software over Comprehensive Documentation)

How often do we work on tasks that are not adding real value, tasks that we just do because things were always done in a certain way? For example, for decades, our department submitted a weekly report to the manager and the manager condensed it and sent it to their manager, and so on. It was well-known that no one read the weekly report and no one understood its purpose, so the quality of what was submitted was dismal, to say the least. But we did it anyway.

The same is true for the time that corporate leaders and management consultants spend on perfecting PowerPoint slides, as if producing slides is progress. Yes, these slides contain important information, but we shouldn't be focusing on the slide design and forgetting our real goals. Agile leadership incorporates the Lean Startup methodology, where we focus on tasks that are moving the needle, actually moving us closer to our goals.

In a software development team, value-adding work is actual programming; in an engineering design firm, it is producing the design models and verifying them to ensure that there are no weaknesses; in a due diligence project, it's the actual analysis that can lead to a decision. If people feel that what they are working on is adding little value to the goal or the desired outcome, they will not feel valuable to the team and their motivation will suffer.

Our job as agile leaders is to make people's jobs meaningful by showing them how their work is contributing to the achievement of the desired outcome. Our job is to show how every piece of the machine is working together to produce results. Employees who know that they are working on meaningful tasks will be more motivated and will perform better, as they know that they are making a difference.

3. Collaboration (Customer Collaboration over Contract Negotiation)

Instead of building systems in which individuals and teams compete, as agile leaders, we build systems in which we maximize collaboration. Collaboration is about having a win-win mindset. It is realizing that, even if we can do this work faster alone, the benefits of doing it with others are far greater. Firstly, collaboration allows us to include wider perspectives, ensuring that our assumptions and our conclusions are challenged and we become aware of our blind spots, leading to more robust solutions. Secondly, the more we collaborate as teams, the more we feel collective ownership of our work. Often, leaders will create a plan and a strategy and pass them on to the team to execute. For more effective execution, try involving the team in the strategic and planning work, allowing them to take full ownership of the process and the outcome.

As agile leaders, our job is to facilitate collaboration, to get the different parts of the system to sync together to produce a coherent and seamless deliverable and outcome. Our job is to help teams break free from the competitive mindset that is deeply ingrained in us and reinforced by performance metrics where employees are stacked against each other. Our job is to build trust in teams so they can effectively collaborate to produce outstanding results.

In chapter 12, "Collaboration," I go into more depth on how to build a collaborative environment and how we can be collaborative leaders.

4. Resilience (Responding to Change over Following a Plan)

Responding to change over following a plan is about building resilience, both in yourself as a leader and in your team. Resilience is about continuously receiving feedback from the team and the customers, adjusting your process, and pivoting as needed. Plans are essential, but we do not stick to them blindly. We adjust and adapt as the environment changes, as we understand the problem more, and as more data is made available. We build systems so that the team can continue working in a sustainable manner and so that, regardless of outside changes, they become independent and autonomous yet maintain high levels of collaboration.

A resilient team is built on pillars of trust, strong relationships, and grit.

As a leader, you are responsible for building a trusting environment where we all know we are working toward a common goal, we have one another's best interests in mind, and we care about each other as people. In a resilient company and team, we invest in relationships and we do what we can to help each other achieve success. We are team players with win-win attitudes, and we support each other. Building resilience is fundamental to team culture and prevents toxic environments at work.

To achieve challenging goals, we need grit. Grit is our ability to face challenges along the way and adapt as needed. It allows us to maintain the passion and perseverance necessary to achieve long-term objectives.

In our workplaces today, change is constant. An agile leader works to make sure that the team can manage the changes and deal with novel scenarios and to ensure that they are developing the skills needed to deal with setbacks and move on.

Chapter 15 is focused on building your resilience as a person and as a leader using the same pillars of trust, strong relationships, and grit, that you use to build resilience within your team.

Now that we understand the values on which agile leadership is built, let's dive into why agile leadership is effective not just for software development teams but for all teams.

When we successfully implement agile leadership, we create autonomy and drive creativity and growth. That is the ultimate purpose, and it is important to keep in mind in our leadership journey.

Autonomy

Agile leadership allows for autonomy within a team. Autonomy means that individuals and teams are self-driven and given independence and authority to make decisions about their roles.

Autonomous teams need clarity on the direction they are headed in order to be successful, and as a leader, you continuously facilitate this process. You do not tell them exactly what to do, but rather make decisions together in such a way that everyone can buy in. When your team feels trusted, is part of the decision-making process, and has autonomy over how they do the work, it becomes easier for them to take ownership of the outcomes.

Autonomy Drives Creativity

Creativity is and will continue to be the most important attribute of a successful workforce in the postindustrial era, particularly as technology and AI replace a lot of the repetitive and analytical tasks we perform at work. Yet we undervalue creativity in our work environments today. We hold outdated schemas, labeling kids either "creative" or "brainy" even from a very early age, as if the two are mutually exclusive and "creative" kids are destined for different paths. We forget that creativity is just as important when designing complex engineering solutions and working in the lab developing vaccines as it is when writing books or painting portraits—and, on the other hand, an analytical mind is just as important when devising a plot for a film as it is when doing advanced financial forecasting. Regardless of the field you are in, you can benefit from both the logical left brain and the intuitive and creative right brain.

The more autonomy you give to your team, the more creativity will thrive. To create autonomy, leaders need to lead and not direct. If you give too many directions on how a task should be done or which task your team should do, they will lose accountability and ownership. Instead, hold people accountable to the outcomes that you have set together and then give them the freedom to figure it out. I like to get out of my team's way so that they can use their brains to figure out the best way to meet the outcomes that I'm looking for. That is when I see a team's creativity blossom.

Work is the place to be creative. The most important challenge for us as leaders is how to transform our current linear, process-oriented workplaces to multidimensional, human-centric, innovative arenas where the imagination has no bounds and everything is possible, where every individual can bring their most creative self to work.

Now more than ever is when we need to think about what makes us uniquely human, what part of us cannot be replaced by a machine or an algorithm. Our strength as humans is the part of our brain that is responsible for sensing, intuition, creativity, and emotions. It's our ability to connect with other humans and communicate in empathetic ways, sensing the emotions in the room and assessing the qualitative, societal, and environmental impact of our decisions. All these human attributes make us more than cogs in the machine, but rather intelligent, empowered participants in the system.

Why Giving Autonomy Is Hard

A young woman in my team was struggling with her deliverables. I decided to step in and help her. I thought, *I have more experience, so let me help her by sharing my process with her.* She began doing the work my way, and she became more efficient and was meeting the deadlines. But when her next new project came along, she looked to me to hand her the process. I realized my mistake. I thought I had been helping her when I handed her my process, but it had only made her more reliant on me.

Being a leader is coaching someone through the problem instead of simply handing them the answer. If we want to create autonomy, we have to be patient. We have to coach them by asking questions, helping them come up with the solutions themselves. Even if the young woman had come up with a process that was less efficient than mine, it would have been her process, and she would have had ownership. When I took over, I was indirectly giving her the message that I could not trust her to come up with a process herself. In Norwegian, we use the term *mestringsfølelse*, which translates to "feeling of mastery" or "feeling of accomplishment." If I had been patient and had let her attempt her process and iterate on it (with my guidance), she would have gotten that feeling of mastery that is so essential in building a young person's confidence.

We think we are being efficient when we just tell our team members how something is done, instead of letting them figure it out and make mistakes. But is it really efficiency when your team becomes dependent on you to solve their problems? Efficiency is no longer every incremental output we can produce. Efficiency is about building a high-performance team that is autonomous, driven, and creative! A team that can devise its own solutions over the long term.

Empathy and Compassion

Once, after I received surprise critical feedback from my boss, I was feeling insecure about my leadership. I mentioned my feelings to my husband, and he responded, "Nada, you just spent the weekend taking the kids with you to check in on one of your team members because you realized that she is all alone in her apartment during the severe lockdown. How many bosses have you had who would have done that for you?"

Empathy and compassion are important values of mine, and I believe that, to be an effective leader, you must listen to your team and see the world through their eyes. My husband's words were a great reminder that I was showing up as a leader even if my boss had critical feedback on other aspects of my performance.

As a leader, I spend a lot of time reflecting on how I can show up with more empathy and compassion. There are simple ways that we can do this that can have a huge impact on our team culture. I, for example, regularly check in with my team, asking them how they are doing—and then listening, really listening. I don't think about my next meeting or to-do item. I stay curious, and I ask questions. It is my job as a leader to know when my team needs help and support; however, if I don't listen and ask good questions, I will never know.

I also make time to do nice things for the team, things as simple as sending flowers on a team member's birthday or celebrating a new project they helped the company win. Bake a cake, or take them out for dinner. We are all people, after all, and it is important to show that you care about your team members' well-being.

Empathy means realizing when people need a break or when they may be going through a tough time. Everyone is doing the best they can. Extend that deadline if it's not super critical. Be better at prioritizing the team's workload, and show that you respect their time.

Growth

I will never forget the words of caution from my mentor when I took on my first leadership role:

"Now you must focus on your team's growth over your own."

This was a moment of profound introspection for me. As a competitive go-getter, I was overtly focused on my growth and my growth alone. Now, I had to shift my focus and prioritize my team.

As a leader, your goal is to help your team grow so that your business can grow and you can grow as a leader. If your leadership is grounded in agile values, growth will be an inevitable outcome.

My ability to prioritize my team's growth was put to test when my boss came to me with an exciting M&A (Mergers and Acquisitions) project that was underway and asked if I would like to lead it. I had been wanting to be more involved in M&A work, and this was the perfect opportunity for me to learn. But my mentor's powerful words kept on coming back to me.

Even though I was personally interested in the project and knew that taking it would give me an opportunity for career advancement, I knew that I would also grow as a leader if I was able to prioritize my team's growth and exposure over my own. I paused, reflected, and decided to pass on the project to someone on my team. While I was disappointed to lose out on the opportunity for myself, I knew that I had chosen what was right for me as a leader.

As a leader, my focus is on building a high-performance team, not just executing the tasks on our to-do lists. I want to make sure that I am not that boss who is unable to share the workload and responsibility with her team, especially when I know they are ready to take it on. I am wary never to become the boss who does not effectively delegate and is perpetually overworked, to the extent that she does not have time for her team. I have had my share of overworked bosses who would snap at me for knocking on their doors because they were just too busy.

I make a conscious effort to not be that kind of boss, to say no to project work if it is going to take me away from my role as a manager. Instead, I find ways to get my team involved in projects so that they can grow and I get to free up time.

Leading in this way means that, instead of presenting to the board, I give the opportunity to someone new. Instead of leading that exciting new project, I give that responsibility to the other upcoming talents in my organization. Instead of doing everything, I delegate more, and that includes delegating decision-making and giving away responsibility to others who are craving it. That is how my team grows, and when my team grows, I grow.

I think about the younger me, who was eager to get more challenging work. I wanted to get involved in strategic projects or get more customer-facing responsibility, and I had the desire to use my analytical and creative brain. But I felt stuck in my current role and responsibilities, and I did not know how to break into those new roles.

Now, as a leader, I am on the lookout for employees who are feeling the way that my younger self used to feel. My job is to find work that will satiate that hunger and drive. Helping your team grow is hard, but it is essential to your role as a leader. Sometimes, you are a teacher, but mostly, you are the coach. You are not solving all problems for your team, but you are ensuring that you present them with the right problems and create the right environment where they will be driven and motivated to solve them. How well your team does is a reflection of you.

A leader leads by getting work accomplished through others. A leader motivates and inspires the team toward an exciting vision and works on building a culture where high-performance is possible and where everyone is growing and performing.

Agile leadership is the leadership of the future, where the world is more automated and highly dependent on the critical thinking of the human brain. Directive and controlling leadership worked well for the factory floor and may still work in certain parts of organizations, but I believe that the power of agile leadership outweighs the benefits of a highly controlled organization. Agile leaders decentralize power, allow their teams to take ownership by making decisions, and build trust through minimal micromanagement, thereby giving way to autonomy and growth. They make space for their teams to be creative, experiment with new ways of working, and adapt quickly. To function in this way, agile leaders ensure open communication, as things change fast as you iteratively and collaboratively move forward toward your goal.

Leaders are not born, they are built. We become leaders through constant practice, training, and hard work. You can become the leader that you have always wanted to be; it is a choice. The only prerequisite is a genuine interest in helping others grow to reach ambitious goals.

Hopefully, you are now inspired to start applying these agile principles to your leadership style. As you build trust and start giving your team more autonomy, you will notice that they will take more initiative and start to devise more efficient ways of working. The team will also appear less stressed as they build resilience from being able to solve hard challenges and begin to trust their ability to do so in the future. They will be motivated to contribute as they take ownership for meeting the goals.

In the following chapters, you will learn how you can create more opportunities for yourself in your career and how you can practice agile leadership at more influential levels in order to make real business impact.

First, though, let's dive into what being a woman has to do with it.

Chapter 4:

Being a Woman

Women belong in all places where decisions are made.
It shouldn't be that women are the exception.

— *Ruth Bader Ginsburg*

How many times have you heard women talk about being the only woman in a room?

I used to do so often myself. But one day, I began to sense the subtle pride in those words. *I made it against all the odds. I am a warrior.* The phrase began to irritate me slightly.

It began to sound like "Look at me, being that one woman who persevered in this cutthroat male-dominated industry! I figured out the game. I got accepted into the club. What an accomplishment!"

When I got promoted to middle management, I became aware of the system that is keeping women from staying in higher roles and moving further upward. As I climbed the ladder, I realized how much everyone was expected to behave and work the same way. Since I was working in a male-dominated industry, the standards had been set by men. Could it be that women were falling out *not* because they did not want to work as much or because they would rather be doing something else, but because this way of working is not designed for women at all?

It sounds obvious now, but I had a small moment of epiphany that day. I realized that I subscribed to the delusion that all we had to do was fit in, act like the other male leaders, and show that we had what it takes. I had believed that I would be that warrior, that Wonder Woman savior, one of the few who figured out the game and broke through the glass ceiling.

This realization, that at some subconscious level I thought I was better than other women, made me livid. All this time, had I actually been thinking that things would be different for me? Was I trying to prove that I could play the game, that other women were not willing to play and that that was why they were not in the room with me?

I was embarrassed.

I needed some serious reframing in my subconscious mind. There is nothing to be proud of about being the only woman in the room. It is not a badge of honor. It is an artifact of an outdated system that women were purposely kept out of for centuries. The game needs to change, not the women.

I realized how empty my accomplishments were if I was not changing the system to include women, if I was simply fitting in to climb the ranks and could not lead in my own unique, feminine way. I realized that being the only woman in the room was the problem, not the solution.

I am not better than other women. There are many women who are just as deserving—or even more deserving—but the systematic bias keeps them from entering the room. The system was not designed with women in mind. With this book, I want to give a voice to women in corporate, women in male-dominated environments, in places where we are a minority. I talk about how the masculine structures and systems we have built have impacted me, how men and women can benefit from balancing the masculine and feminine inside of us, how I need to stop suppressing and undervaluing the feminine. These are mostly my reflections and stories, but they are largely influenced by women I have met on this journey who have taught me so much about vulnerability, staying true to ourselves, finding self-worth, and resisting the urge to fit in.

For those of you who are feeling stuck, I want to show you that there are alternative paths and alternative role models that can lead you to achieve success that's designed for you, taking your values and your strengths into account. When you are able to fully express yourself, that is when your true power is revealed.

How did we get here?

For centuries, our work environment has been dominated by men. During the industrial revolution, women were relegated to household affairs and men were the breadwinners; for better or for worse, the responsibilities for bringing in enough for their families lay solely on their shoulders. The workplace was designed for men because it was the sole domain of men. Now, though, in the modern day, women have entered the workplace, and we are gradually figuring out what needs to change to create space for us. It is hard to preempt changes even when, in retrospect, they seem obvious.

This issue reminds me of an exchange from the movie *Hidden Figures*, which recounts the story of three African American, Katherine Johnson, Dorothy Vaughan and Mary Jackson, working at NASA in the 1960s. In one scene, Katherine Johnson's boss at NASA reprimands her for taking long breaks, but she tells him that she has no other choice because "there's no bathroom for me here." Her boss is baffled because he had not even noticed this problem. She elaborates, "There is no bathroom. There are no colored bathrooms in this building. Or any building outside the West Campus, which is half a mile away. Did you know that? I have to walk to Timbuktu just to relieve myself. And I can't use one of the handy bikes . . . And I work like a dog, day and night, living off of coffee from a pot none of you wanna touch! So excuse me if I have to go to the restroom a few times a day."

At play in this scene is the intersectionality of race and gender in a segregated society and the stark gap in the reality of a white man and an African American woman. It shows how a privileged person whose basic needs are met can be blatantly oblivious to the unmet needs of others who are less privileged. We assume that, now that we allow women to work, everything will sort itself out on its own. But that's not the case. Gender equality at work is taking too long, and the current estimate is that it will take another ninety-nine years to close the gap in the workplace. Deep inherent biases, even if they seem subtle, have grave consequences to diversity participation in the workplace.

The pay gap is one example that is easily quantifiable. Women continue to earn less than men for doing the same work, with the average woman earning only 82 cents for every dollar earned by a man. This pay gap is even wider for women of color, with Black women earning just 79 cents and Hispanic women earning only 78 cents for every dollar earned by a white man.[3] In addition, women face other barriers in the workplace, such as lack of access to high-paying industries and senior leadership positions. According to the 2022 McKinsey & Company Women in the Workplace report, for every one hundred men promoted and hired to manager, only seventy-two women are promoted and hired. This broken rung results in more women getting stuck at the entry level,

---

3   "2022 State of the Gender Pay Gap Report," Payscale, accessed January 24, 2023, *https://www.payscale.com/research-and-insights/gender-pay-gap/*.

and fewer women becoming managers. Not surprisingly, men end up holding 62 percent of manager-level positions, while women hold just 38 percent. This disparity is even more pronounced for women of color and LGBT women, who face additional barriers such as discrimination and bias.

Women of color face higher rates of microaggressions compared to white women as well as more barriers for advancement. Microaggressions are subtle, often unintentional actions or comments that reinforce negative stereotypes or marginalize individuals based on their race, gender, sexuality, or other identity. The Women in the Workplace report found that women of color are more ambitious despite getting less support: according to the report, "41 percent of women of color want to be top executives, compared with 27 percent of white women." Yet that ambition does not translate into career advancement the way it does for men and even for white women.[4] In devising systems that effectively promote equity and inclusion for all women, it is critical to be aware of intersectionality and the fact that people have more than one identity based on which they can be discriminated against.

We must work together to uproot these biases and bring them to the surface, and we shouldn't be afraid to talk about the issues we confront. We choose not to bring up microaggressions and subtle biases because they seem

---

4   Alexis Krivkovich et al. "Women in the Workplace 2022," McKinsey & Company, October 18, 2022, https://www.mckinsey.com/featured-insights/diversity-and-inclusion/women-in-the-workplace.

insignificant and commonplace. We do not want to develop reputations as complainers, over-exaggerators, or victims. We want to overlook these things and just get on with our work; we feel that we cannot get hung up on everything. While there is truth to that—we cannot get engulfed in the negative and lose sight of our goals—if we do not address these issues, they will continue to persist and the gap will take even longer to close.

Is our workplace designed for women?

I became concerned with this question a few years ago, when I was promoted to head of research and innovation while I was pregnant. I had bad morning sickness and being in the office before 11 a.m. was pure torture. Our offices were in a fancy new building with plenty of spacious, neatly designed break areas next to the coffee machines. Most of these spaces were usually unoccupied. I went down to the facility's office and asked if there was a resting room for pregnant women. They did not know. They said there was a prayer room on one of the floors. Engulfed with nausea, I wandered all the floors in search of a room where I could lie down. I could not find one. I did find the prayer room, though, a neat room with a carpet and a man in prayer position. The company had a prayer room, but no nursing room or room where pregnant women (or others with special needs) could lie down? We, an organization employing over 4,000 women, had not thought about that.

Caroline Criado Perez wrote a book on this exact topic, *Invisible Women: Data Bias in a World Designed for Men.*

In her research, she found that most things are "one size fits men," from smartphones to car safety to medical trials.

Perez uses data to show how we live in a man's world, and men did not bake in gender differences while building it. The optimum office temperature was developed based on the metabolic resting rate of a "reference man." It is no surprise then that most women bundle up with extra scarves and sweaters at the office since the temperatures are five degrees too cold for women. Data showed that even today, women are being misdiagnosed and dying because symptoms of heart attacks or other diseases do not present the same way in women as they do in men (medical trials generally use male participants). Cars are designed for the body of "Reference Man," a twenty-five to thirty-year-old male weighing 154 pounds, standing 5 feet 6 inches tall, Caucasian, with a Western European or North American lifestyle. Therefore, women involved in collisions are nearly 50 percent more likely to be seriously hurt, as the safety systems did not consider the physiological differences between men and women.[5]

The "Reference Man," which was first introduced in 1975 to simplify calculations in research on humans, is in fact still used for many products that are put on the market today.[6]

---

5   Caroline Criado Perez, Invisible Women: Exposing Data Bias in a World Designed for Men (Broadway, NY: Abrams Press, 2019).

6   "Report of the Task Group on Reference Man," Annals of the ICRP 3, no. 1–4 (1975): iii, *https://doi.org/10.1016/0146-6453(79)90123-4*.

I was curious about how the "one size fits men" idea applied in other ways, beyond structural design. How about the entire workplace culture, the schedules, the value systems, the performance systems, and the leadership styles? How different would the workplace be if it hadn't been built for men? Everything was set up in the way that men figured was ideal for them. And when I say this, I am not alluding to some giant conspiracy by powerful men to keep women deliberately at a disadvantage. I am just highlighting that, because women were mostly out of the picture when the earlier versions of office workplaces were designed in the preindustrial and industrial era, we have not been able to seriously consider the needs of women (and a diverse workforce in general). Throughout this book, I work on answering these very questions, as I believe that our way of working would be radically different if women were also part of defining the workplace.

Men and women are designed differently by nature. Our bodies, including our brains, are wired differently. Hormones in our bodies determine how we think, feel, and, ultimately, behave. Men and women have very different compositions of hormones that circulate in our bodies. For men, the composition does not change from day to day the way it does for a woman. Women are on a monthly cycle.

Our physiology, our energy level, and our moods change depending on where we are on our hormonal cycles. When our hormone levels plummet right before and during our periods, our bodies are exhausted from being on high alert, getting ready for a fertilized egg. Our bodies are busy making changes to get back to normal. After our periods, we enter the follicular phase, when estrogen and testosterone levels begin to build again. These hormones may cause us to have a heightened sense of smell, along with clear thinking and better coordination. Many women report feeling their best at this time of the month. Imagine presenting to the board during this phase (versus right before your period!). We experience huge variation in our energy levels based on what is going on in our bodies.

In a masculine work environment, we value consistency above all. Could this high value on consistency be preventing us from reaching the true excellence that can come from being more in tune with our bodies? Could there be actual benefits to our workplaces if we took advantage of when we were feeling the most creative and energized? Are there ways of making our workplace more flexible so we can accommodate women's cycles of energy? Could we devise systems that allow variation in performance and energy levels instead of expecting perfection every single time?

Women spend a third of our lives in peri- or postmenopause, yet menopause is still a taboo topic, and there is very little research on how it impacts women in the workplace. Menopause hits women when they are often at the peak of their careers, in their late forties or early fifties. The symptoms can be minor to debilitating, including memory problems, fatigue, and increased anxiety. A survey of 2,000 women from ages forty-five to sixty-seven experiencing menopause symptoms in the UK found that lack of support at the workplace is having a direct impact on women's choices to leave the workplace.[7] Women said that menopause had the second most devastating impact on their careers that they had experienced in their lifetimes, only just behind having children. This is devastating for women who have given their work all they have for their entire lives and want to continue working but do not receive any meaningful support to keep on working in a way that allows them to cope with the symptoms. Menopause is a natural part of a women's life course and shouldn't mean the end of their career, but in many instances, it does. A survey in the US found that 17 percent of 1,010 women in menopause have quit a job or considered quitting due to symptoms that interfere with their work performance or productivity on a weekly basis.[8]

In a world where we choose to stay ignorant of these variations, oblivious to the changes in our biology, we find fault in ourselves. We feel guilty for being inconsistent and not having the stamina to maintain productivity and concentration levels during the month. We fear being labeled—and we tend ⟨

---

7   Amelia Hill, "More than 1m UK Women Could Quit Their Jobs through Lack of Menopause Support," The Guardian, January 17, 2022, https://www. theguardian.com/society/2022/jan/17/more-than-1m-uk-women-could-quit-their-jobs-through-lack-of-menopause-support.

8   "Biote Women in the Workplace Survey," Biote, last updated May 10, 2022, *https://biote.com/learning-center/biote-women-in-the-workplace-survey*.

to label each other as moody, erratic, all over the place and confused. When I notice that these feelings are creeping in for me, I realize I am trying to live up to an ideal of a person who is a man, a man's mind and body.

Demystifying the Masculine and the Feminine Labels

Yin and yang, male and female, strong and weak, rigid and tender, heaven and hell, light and darkness, thunder and lightning, cold and warmth, good and evil . . . the interplay of opposite principles constitutes the universe.

— *Confucius*

Equality in the workplace does not mean that men and women are treated the same; it is about equity, recognizing our differences not only as men and women, but as individuals, so we can devise ways to leverage those differences to produce our best work.

I spent most of my career staying indifferent to the masculine and feminine parts of me. I tried to just fit in, which I realize now meant showing up in the masculine.

Rita, one of my coaches, gave me the vocabulary to better understand the masculine and the feminine within us. I was a bit hesitant to use those terms because of preconceived ideas of what they meant and the polarization they can create. Notions of the masculine and the feminine are often dismissed in our cultures, as if they are binary, as if one is better than the other. It is contentious and can be easily misunderstood.

Let me explain what I mean by the feminine and the masculine. The masculine is usually associated with the left brain, which is the more logical and analytical side of the brain, and the feminine is associated with the right brain. This part of the brain is superior at spatial awareness, imagination, and recognizing patterns. Men and women both have both the masculine and feminine within them.

In the Western world, the different characteristics of the brain were termed *masculine* and *feminine* by Carl Jung, the Swiss psychiatrist and psychoanalyst. He called them the *anima* and the *animus* as the ancient archetypes of *eros* (female) and *logos* (male). From ancient times, the eros, or the female, has been associated with receptivity, creativity, relationships, and wholeness, whereas the logos has been said to be connected to power, thought, and action. In Chinese medicine and philosophy, the yin and the yang have existed for much longer, as have the Shiva and the Shakti in Hindu mythology. *Yin*, the feminine energy, is supposed to be gentle, receptive, intuitive, and fulfilling, whereas *yang*, the masculine, is active, fast, fierce, emptying, goal-oriented, and focused. The focus of Eastern medicine has always been on balancing the yin and the yang, the polar energies, to avoid imbalance.

Feminine and masculine characteristics are not science; these are mere associations, culturally determined, that have been passed down over generations. While again, historically, in Eastern and Western cultures, the qualities of the left brain have been associated with men and the qualities of the right brain have been associated with women, we are not necessarily either more "left-brained" or "right-brained" based on our gender. There are plenty of women who operate more in their left brains and plenty of men who operate in their right brains. There is no scientific evidence that some people use more of their left hemispheres or their right hemispheres. The brain is interconnected, and both hemispheres support each other in the brain's processes and functions. We do, however, tend to see that some people are more analytical while others are more creative.

We all have both masculine and feminine energy within us. They are simply metaphors for different ways of thinking and operating, which some may refer to as the left and the right hemispheres of the brain. When I am sitting down and focusing on a complex calculation, I am operating in my left brain, masculine energy. I am focused; I am using my analytical brain. When I get up and go take a shower and experience a eureka moment about how I can solve a tough problem, it is my right brain, the feminine, that is activated.

This is no way meant to characterize men or women in a certain way or get them to fit into boxes. It is more to underscore how our workplaces value certain ways of being more than others, creating an imbalance that negatively impacts women and diversity in general.

Scientific Research on Cognitive Differences

There is plenty of scientific research on differences in behavior and cognitive ability between men and women. Diane Halpern, a scientist at Claremont McKenna College, looked at all the research published on the matter and saw that there is significant research pointing to the biological basis of sex-based cognitive differences.

According to *Stanford Medicine Magazine's* review of her findings:

> Women excel in several measures of verbal ability— pretty much all of them, except for verbal analogies. Women's reading comprehension and writing ability consistently exceed that of men, on average. They outperform men in tests of fine-motor coordination and perceptual speed. They're more adept at retrieving information from long-term memory.

> Men, on average, can more easily juggle items in working memory. They have superior visuospatial skills: They're better at visualizing what happens when a complicated two- or three-dimensional shape is rotated in space, at correctly determining angles from the horizontal, at tracking moving objects and at aiming projectiles.

This research suggests that our brains do work differently, though our brains are more similar than dissimilar and these differences show up most at extremes. Even if this data is scientifically significant, scientists would caution against making gross generalizations, as there are huge variations within genders.[9]

I am uncomfortable boxing men and women into gender-specific strengths, yet I believe that it is important to be aware of them in the context of our workplace and what we have come to value. A better approach is to think in terms of allowing the masculine and the feminine to coexist and valuing all the strengths equally. This will make more space for women who do operate differently, as shown by research and data.

Masculine and the Feminine in the Workplace

We have built structures that are tilted toward the left brain, where we value structure, linear thinking (to-do lists and hierarchies), control, assertiveness, and analytical thinking. We undervalue characteristics that are associated with the right brain, and we often refer to these characteristics as *soft skills*: creativity, compassion, communication, intuition, collaboration, and perceptiveness. Since women tend to exhibit right-brain characteristics, we tend to be better at reading the room due to our ability to read facial expressions and body language more accurately. That is a great asset to have during negotiation, just as important as being able to do mental calculations at the negotiation table.

---

9   Bruce Goldman, "Two Minds: The Cognitive Differences between Men and Women," Stanford Medicine Magazine, Spring 2017, *https://stanmed.stanford. edu/how-mens-and-womens-brains-are-different/*.

A workplace that is designed for diversity would equally value all these traits, and both men and women who don't fit the norm will benefit.

For example, in our linear, left-brain-dominant world, we are told to focus on one thing to achieve more success. One day I was listening to Marie Forleo, an entrepreneur and coach, talk about having multiple passions, like, dance, business, and teaching and how each one of her passions in some way benefits her other passions. They balance who she is.[10] It dawned on me that we live in a world where the conventional wisdom is to find one thing we are passionate about, our reason for being, and laser focus on it to achieve success in our lives. But there is also wisdom in holding multiple passions. When we do, we can zoom in and out as desired, depending on the phase of our lives, the time of day, or simply our mood. We can have a fuller, more enhanced experience of life in which different parts of us come alive. When you give space to the feminine, you can hold multiple passions, combine them, mix them up, and enrich different parts of you.

Microaggressions

A friend once commented that women can get a bit aggressive at work. *Aggressive* is a label often given to women if they step outside of what is the expected norm from them.

---

10   Steven Bartlett, interview with Marie Forleo, "E184: World Leading Life Coach: 3 Steps To Figuring Out ANYTHING You Want: Marie Forleo," October 5, 2022, in *The Diary Of A CEO with Steven Bartlett*, podcast, MP3 audio, 1:33:49, https://podcasts.apple.com/gb/podcast/the-diary-of-a-ceo-with-steven-bartlett/id1291423644.

Aggression is seen as out of character for women, but in men, it is easily overlooked. I tried to explain to my friend that if a woman is repeatedly dismissed, interrupted, talked over, ignored, alienated, and belittled, it makes sense for that to manifest in some way. The woman might eventually snap at you or start to assert a boundary. When those around her are not used to that, it is easy to label those reactions as aggressiveness.

A few years ago, I was assigned to be tender manager for a big client, and I had to work with a VP (let's call him Val), who had previously been dismissive toward me in our interactions. At one point, I found myself sitting in an all-day workshop that Val and his team were also attending. During a break, Val came up to me and said, "Nada, we have a lot of work to do on the tender. Shouldn't you be working on that?"

I was a bit surprised, as Val was not my manager. I simply told him that I was waiting for input from his team, who were also in the workshop. He took out his laptop and gave me a very specific task: he told me to leave the workshop and instead make an Excel spreadsheet with what was missing and who was responsible.

It was not what I wanted to do, but I agreed. I assumed that the task would take me thirty minutes, and we would be going on lunch break soon. I skipped lunch, finished the spreadsheet, shipped it to Val, and made my way back to the workshop. A few minutes in, he walked across the room, tapped me on the shoulder, and signaled me to step outside.

"I looked through the spreadsheet. It's great. You've identified tasks that you can be working on right now."

He gave me a fake smile as he put his hands on his hips to assume his *power pose.* I could have very easily felt small in that moment, as his tall, broad frame stood in between me and the door to the workshop. I looked up slowly so my eyes could meet his. I was not an intern or a fresh graduate. I considered myself to be Val's equal and equally eligible for his role, given my experience. Yet he saw me as a petite young woman who needed to be told what to do and how to spend her time.

The optics were horrible for my rebellious feminist ego. I was enraged. I looked Val dead in the eyes and said sternly, "Val, I am waiting for input from your team. They are sitting right there in that workshop. If they can wait to do the work, then so can I! I am going back in."

Val raised his eyebrows as I charged past him, causing him to lose his footing in his not-so-sturdy-anymore power pose.

I was furious.

Did I react in an aggressive manner? Boy, was I mad!

I stood up for myself, and, for anyone who didn't know the context of the situation, that may have seemed like an overreaction.

I do not know if his treatment was linked to my gender, my age, or the fact that I was the only woman and person of color in the room. That is the challenge with microaggressions—they are so subtle that we dismiss them, giving the aggressor rather than the person who experiences them the benefit of the doubt. What bystanders do not see are the accumulations of microaggressions that result in such a response. Val had been dismissive to me from our very first interaction.

In hindsight, I could have reacted better and not let this man's poor leadership get the better of me. I could have smiled and not gotten angry but still told him that I would work on the tender later, then gone back into the meeting. Or, even better, I could have sought help, enlisted allies at work, and perhaps even talked to Val one-on-one about how he was making me feel. But I cannot put the burden solely on my shoulders to fix the microaggressions I face. I am dependent on others believing my experience (I will come back to this in chapter 9, "Diversity, Equity, and Inclusion"). I find comfort in the words of Ruchika Tulshyan, a diversity and inclusion advocate and the author of the book *Inclusion on Purpose*, who says that if you experience microaggressions, "It is never your responsibility to fix it. Speak up if you feel safe. Look for upstanders after the interaction who might be able to speak to the person. Most of all: know that it is never, never your fault or in your head."[11]

---

11   Ruchika Tulshyan, "This question directed to Prime Ministers Jacinda Ardern (NZ) and Sanna Marin (Finland) was so offensive but a reminder of the daily aggressions women face," LinkedIn, accessed January 24, 2023, *https://www.linkedin.com/posts/rtulshyan_this-question-directed-to-prime-ministers-activity-7003760128684408832-UvXV/*.

I let my experience with Val impact me profoundly, in a way that I wish I hadn't. I ruminated over it for far too long, and it made me angry. Why did I get so triggered? Why did I let someone from the outside put me so out of balance that it impacted my work? I really did not want rebellion and victimhood to become part of who I was as an ambitious woman. But in that moment, I wanted to rebel against his behavior, and I felt like a victim.

I do not want to be angry. It takes precious energy away from my purpose. I want to lead with compassion even in the face of injustice, the way Nelson Mandela did. *He* did not lead from a place of self-righteousness or a desire to right a wrong. Instead, he led from a place of love:

> No one is born hating another person because of the colour of his skin, or his background, or his religion. People must learn to hate, and if they can learn to hate, they can be taught to love, for love comes more naturally to the human heart than its opposite.[12]

I once came across a post on social media recounting a story about a monk who decides to take a boat to the middle of a lake, away from everyone else, to meditate. As he falls deeper into his meditation, he feels another boat hitting him. He keeps his eyes closed and starts to get really annoyed. His anger builds up. *Can't this other guy see that I am meditating?*

---

12   Nelson Mandela, Long Walk to Freedom (Little, Brown and Company, 1994).

What is wrong with him? Finally, it gets to a point where he must open his eyes so he can yell at the other person. He is surprised to see that there is nobody there. An empty boat had made its way to the middle of lake, and the waves are causing it to gently rock against his boat. In that moment, he realizes that he himself is the true source of anger, not someone external.[13]

Just like this monk, anger resides in me, and I let someone like Val provoke it. Sometimes it's Val, while other times it's someone else. This got me thinking, *How long am I going to live at the mercy of an empty boat knocking into me? Why am I choosing to take the burden of all of womanity when someone is mean to me? What if it has nothing to do with my gender, nothing to do with me, but everything to do with the person who is provoking me?*

Does being angry help me in my quest for more equality in the workplace? Perhaps it does. Anger makes us strive for change. Yet I do not want to live my life in angry rebellion. I do not want to waste my life living in resentment, striving for an unobtainable ideal of fairness and justice. I must find a different path. There are two sides to every story, and sometimes the best thing I can do to drive change is to lead with forgiveness.

---

13   *Adapted from* Thích Nhất Hạnh, Being Peace (Berkeley, California: Parallax Press, 1987), 32.

Motherhood and Ambition

When I called the VP of HR to let her know that I was resigning from my new VP role that was given to me after my dream role was restructured away, she said, "Nada, you are a mother with two young kids. I completely understand that you are quitting. I did the same when I was in your phase of life."

That was the last thing that I wanted to hear. There were many reasons why I had decided to leave, but being a mom was not one of them. In some indirect way, motherhood might have given me the wisdom and the courage to go ahead with the decision, but it was not the reason I was leaving.

The truth is that I have never thought that motherhood would get in the way of my career. I grew up with a mother who had a full-fledged career while she was raising three kids. She did not sacrifice her ambitions for us. Instead, she gave us all the love in the world, while modeling that one should never put their dreams on hold.

As I write this book, I am reflecting on all the times over the past five years when others at work brought up that I was a mom and I never did. I never felt the need to. I never thought about it. I saw men around me proudly talking about being dads when they introduced themselves in meetings. I found it odd. I would never introduce myself as a mother in a work meeting. It would almost be like me saying I am a sister, daughter, wife, whatever. The fact that I am a mom does not matter. It is not why I am in the meeting.

Even while writing this book, one of my coaches asked me why my book didn't focus on being a mom and a leader. I thought, *Because it is irrelevant.* Being a mother is not relevant to my leadership story. It is just another role I play. Being a mother is nothing out of the ordinary.

But it got me thinking. Somehow, others think that being a mother should be relevant. They want me to talk about the stereotypical struggles of balancing motherhood and a demanding career. They want me to talk about the limits motherhood puts on our careers. But I believe that motherhood only limits us to the extent that we believe it does. It is the system that does not accommodate parents that limits us. It's other people's perceptions and judgments that limit us.

At work, motherhood defines me in other people's reality. They want to see me as a mother. Oh, she is late today— she's a mom. Oh, she can't join this meeting after work—she is a mom. Oh, she can't travel—she is a mom. Oh, she is pushing back on more work—she is a mom.

It is convenient to assume that we leave our jobs, our careers, our dreams to raise our families. It is more easily digestible and a comfortable justification to let go of responsibility, let the status quo persist, and obscure the true reasons why women leave the workplace. We leave our jobs not because we want to, but because we have to or we are made to. We not only did not design the workplace for women, we did not design it for parents.

It was the birth of my first child that made me even more ambitious at work. As I pushed out a baby, it ignited a fire in my belly. If I was to spend eight hours a day away from my baby, my job had to be worth it. It had to be rewarding and meaningful. I was hell-bent on making sure that the mom title would not get in the way of my future C-suite titles. I was meant to do more, and motherhood was only going to propel me forward. The fire made me relentless, engulfing anything that came in my way as I set out to climb the proverbial ladder. I was determined to show that I could be a mother, be who I was, and still have immense success in my career. I was going to be the role model I was looking for.

Early in my career, I subscribed to the thinking that women have to "want it enough." *We are choosing to not enter these very masculine workplaces, and we are choosing to lean back after motherhood.* Coming back to work after having my first child, I realized how wrong I was. I had no intention or desire to lean back. My ambition was stronger than ever before, yet I started to notice the difference in the way I was treated compared to my male colleagues. My ex-Mckinsey boss only wanted to talk analysis with the men, when I was the one who had done the analysis. I would be in the room, trying to get a word in, while my boss and a male colleague would go on and on about the next course of action.

After a while, I noticed that a teammate decided to drop me from out-of-town client meetings. He said that he would take the intern instead. I was aghast. When I confronted him, he said, "Oh, I thought you would not want to go out of town since you have a small child at home." He thought he was just being considerate of my life situation. I explained that I wanted to be part of deciding which meetings I went to and told him that while perhaps I might not travel as much as I had before, the decision was mine to make. He understood completely, and we remain good friends. Instead of getting angry, I got curious and empathetic. Perhaps there is a different way of rebelling?

During this period, I called for an urgent meeting with my mentor. I had recently switched jobs after seven years in the same company. I had barely been in my new role for three months, and it was not going well. I laid out all my frustrations to her and expressed how my career was in shambles. I was thirty-four, and my career was going nowhere. In a desperate attempt to take control, I drew a ten-year timeline on a piece of paper and said to her, "In fifteen years, I am going to be CEO." We started making a plan. How would I get there? What did I need to do?

My wise mentor, Liv Monica Stubholt, is the best ally I have ever had, in particular during such times of desperation. She smiled at me and said, "Why fifteen years? Why not earlier? Why not in ten years or five years?" She knows exactly how to encourage me, but also how to challenge me to think differently and step outside my tunnel vision.

I set the most ambitious goals for myself when I became a mother. I do not believe that it is motherhood that gets in the way of women's career. In fact, it is motherhood that drives us to be the best leaders we can be.

It is not rocket science to design a workplace that accommodates parents. It can be done easily without impacting business operations. Simple measures that worked well during the pandemic without impacting businesses include:

- Flexible working hours,
- Ability to work from home,
- Paid parental leave and sick leave,
- Childcare facilities at work,
- Not putting expectations on parents to work excessive hours, and
- Not basing promotions on face time or number of hours spent on the computer.

Simple measures can have profound impact. When Google increased its maternity leave from twelve weeks to eighteen weeks, it had a direct impact, decreasing turnover rate for young mothers by 50 percent.[14]

Other than these basic measures, there are more nuanced policies that hold mothers back. Take, for example, Norway, a country with affordable childcare and state-mandated parental leave for up to twelve months. There are more ,

---

14   Brigid Schulte et al. "Paid Family Leave: How Much Time Is Enough?," New America, last updated June 16, 2017, https://www.newamerica.org/better-life-lab/reports/paid-family-leave-how-much-time-enough/economic-impact/.

women with small children in paid employment (72 percent) going back to work than in the US, but there are still large discrepancies in pay and the types of jobs that men and women do. Only thirteen of the top 200 companies in Norway are led by women, less than 7 percent.[15] In the biggest pension fund in the world, the infamous Norwegian Oil Fund, women make a lot less compared to men, and only about 16 percent of women are eligible for a yearly bonus (because of the types of jobs they have, usually administrative, and therefore not connected to bonus schemes), according to Norway's biggest business newspaper, *DN*.[16] Furthermore, if parents take more than three months of leave in a year, they are not eligible for a bonus or a raise. This mostly impacts mothers, who are likely to take most of the parental leave in a family, and it discourages fathers from taking any more than three months.

Add to all this the microaggressions and unconscious biases related to motherhood, and no wonder moms are falling behind and deciding to step out of the system that does not

---

15 Ingvild Sagmoen, *"Bare 13 av de nesten 200 selskapene på Oslo Børs styres av kvinner: – Vi har ikke vært gode nok til å jobbe med å få frem kvinner,"* E24, last updated June 23, 2019, https://e24.no/naeringsliv/i/9vxBod/bare-13-av-de-nesten-200-selskapene-paa-oslo-boers-styres-av-kvinner-vi-har-ikke-vaert-gode-nok-til-aa-jobbe-med-aa-faa-frem-kvinner.

16 Åshild Langved and Espen Linderud, *"Kvinnene er lønnstapere i Oljefondet – og de får sjeldnere bonus,"* Dagens Næringsliv, March 7, 2018, https://www.dn.no/marked/norges-bank-investment-management/norges-bank/oljefondet/kvinnene-er-lonnstapere-i-oljefondet-og-de-far-sjeldnere-bonus/2-1-283576.

serve them. They reach a point where the challenges and stress become unsurmountable.

We cannot rely on those who benefit from the current system to drive this change. We need women in positions of power to enact these changes that will benefit society as a whole.

Martin Luther King said, "Darkness cannot drive out darkness; only light can do that. Hate cannot drive out hate, only love can do that."[17] These words are plastered on my wall and came in handy when the words of HR relegated my reason for leaving to motherhood. *I am not going to get angry at her. Her words are simply triggering something inside me, my deep desire to not add to the statistics and not be that woman who leaves her job because of motherhood. Getting angry will not drive change. But me changing my limiting beliefs around who I am and what I am capable of achieving will and can move mountains.*

More on that in the following chapters!

---

17 *Martin Luther King Jr. Strength to Love (Minneapolis: Fortress Press, 1963),* 47.

Chapter 5:
Openness to Learn

If you are not willing to learn, no one can help you. If you are determined to learn, no one can stop you.

— *Zig Ziglar*

Few people land their dream jobs right after college. I was not one of them. I graduated with my master's degree in 2008 and got the only job I could. It was with a small environmental consulting firm in Houston. I joined thinking that I would play my part in protecting the environment, when in fact the firm was probably doing more harm than good.

It was a fifty-person firm, with a president/owner who called all the shots. He hired young graduates, paid them little, and expected them to work sixty-hour weeks. Since it was my first real job, I did as I was told. Your first couple of years working is when your real training happens, and regardless of what job you have, if you are receptive to it, you will learn a lot. It just might not be what you thought you would learn!

I was the new hire, so I was assigned to whatever tasks no one else had the time to do. As a fresh graduate with a thirst for learning, I was okay with that. "Bring it on," I said.

The company needed someone to make geospatial maps showing where the highest concentration of contaminants was found. I became an expert in a geospatial mapping software. It was not the most exciting work, but it made me valuable to the company. I needed to learn some skills, so I did.

The start of one's career can be bumpy. It is normal to not find your footing right away. Many young professionals get hung up and jaded that they did not figure out their careers early, that they missed opportunities, or that they didn't get the jobs they wanted. You take what you get, adopt an agile mindset, and use every opportunity to learn. This is just the beginning, and you have to build on whatever you have in front of you. Make lemonade out of lemons!

In true first-generation-immigrant fashion, that is exactly what I did. I rolled up my sleeves and did the dirty work, whatever it was. It was an opportunity to learn. I did not have an ego yet that would cause me to say no to a boss or to anybody else. I was a sponge, super eager to learn and absorb everything. I was proactive; I raised my hand and helped where needed. I had to build a track record. I had to work hard to leave my mark and get noticed. I had to prove myself.

Everything you learn in your first couple of years working is valuable. Nothing is a waste of time. My first job in college was scooping ice cream at the local Baskin-Robbins. I had just moved to the US, and that job taught me everything I needed to know about American culture and customer service. A kid two years younger than me taught me how to serve, how to talk to people, how to make everyone feel welcomed, how to work as a team during the ice cream rush hour, and how to have a permanent smile plastered on my face regardless of the customers' moods because customer is king. The basics of the American culture!

Focus on Your Natural Talents

If you are lucky, you figure out early on what part of your job comes easily to you. What can you do a lot more quickly than everybody else—or quicker than most people, at least? What part of the job really gives you joy, so much so that you do not see the time go by?

In fact, early on in your career, that is what you should do: explore as much as possible. Ensure that you try out a variety of tasks and experiences. Get curious and get better. If you are someone who has a very analytical mind, who loves working with spreadsheets, hone those skills and become really good at them so that you are the person who is called in every time to analyze and give a point of view. If you are someone who loves to create processes so that there is more structure in your team, use that superpower to do exactly that. Do not wait for permission. Trust me: your team will thank you for it.

Build your career around your strengths to make it more fun and fulfilling and not a continuous uphill battle. Solely focusing on your weak areas is like swimming upstream; there are too many forces working against you.

Have the Courage to Dream Big about Your Career

Once, when I was interviewing for a new position, the hiring manager, Dave, said to me, "I want more women on my leadership team, more women like you who are different." He turned to the head of HR, gave her a contemplative look, and told her, "We should consider her for the VP role we are hiring for."

The head of HR raised her eyebrows, and I could tell that she was not pleased to be having this discussion while I was still in the room. Eventually, she forced a smile and reluctantly said, "Yes, of course."

Dave proceeded to ask me, "How would you feel about taking a VP role? Would you be able to present to the board and talk to our clients' CEOs?"

I was caught off guard, but I knew that the only way to respond was, "Yes, of course! That is what I have always wanted!" I was eager, and I had wanted to take on more responsibility, but I wasn't sure if others would think I had enough experience.

I did not get that role, but Dave planted a seed in my mind. What if I was ready? What if I did not need more learning and more experience to take on more responsibility?

That conversation disrupted one of my limiting beliefs, the belief that I was not ready for a VP role yet. Before that point, I had not considered that I could qualify for such a role. I started believing that I was ready to step up. You have to believe in yourself before others can start believing in you.

From that day onwards, I started to apply for VP positions in the company where I was currently working. No one took me seriously. My boss dissuaded me, but I applied anyway. I was called in for one interview, but I could tell that it was just a play; they already knew who they were hiring. But rejections do not bother me. I think of each rejection as one less rejection in the future, as if the world can only give me a limited number of rejections! I learn from every rejection—they are progress in disguise.

Soon enough, I was interviewing for a VP of innovation position at a leading supplier to the energy industry. They loved me and they wanted to hire me, but not for VP. "We will groom you for the role," they said, and that was good enough to get me to say yes.

For dreams to come true, you must believe in them. I wish I had dreamed bigger earlier, that I had believed in my ability to take on roles with more responsibility without needing someone from the outside to make me aware of it.

If you do not believe in yourself, you are less likely to set ambitious goals. The likelihood of achieving an audacious goal increases significantly when you set the goal and take concrete steps toward it. Do not rely on luck.

Quantum Leap

We perceive our career progress to be incremental, so we keep on taking small steps. Theoretically, if you improved at something 1 percent every day, by the end of the year, you would be thirty-seven times better than when you started. But life is not theoretical and quantifiable in that way. How do you improve 1 percent as a leader every day? It is hard to quantify, but the theory is more about the mindset of growth. The downside of incremental progress is that, over time, we do not even notice the progress we are making or have already made. We are so zoomed in to what lies in front of us, our daily tasks, that we do not see the length we have covered. We get stuck in the learning trap, thinking that we are not ready and we have a lot more to learn. That is why I like the concept of the quantum leap; I believe that we are ready to make big shifts in our lives at any point. *Quantum leap* is a term adapted from chemistry, where an electron jumps from one energy state to another. Figuratively, it means being able to make abrupt change, a sudden increase or dramatic advance. A quantum leap could be going from three years of work experience to VP, or going from VP to CEO. It could be going from presenting to your client to presenting to their board, bringing in $100k a year to bringing in a million dollars the next. Quantum leaps don't happen gradually, but from one day to the next. Believing in quantum leaps is believing that big shifts can happen in an instant. Keep on making that incremental progress, but believe that you are ready for a quantum leap at any point.

How to Set Ambitious Goals

As a singles tennis player, Serena Williams has won twenty-three Grand Slam singles titles, more than any other athlete—female or male. She has also won fourteen Grand Slam doubles titles along with her sister Venus, as well as three gold medals in doubles at the Olympics. She is the highest-earning woman athlete of all time.

How does she do it? By setting ambitious goals for herself. She has a match book where she writes down her goals. For example, she might write, "Win the Grand Slam," "Be the number one in tennis," or "Get the gold or silver."

She is specific. Then she tracks every game and reflects in her match book about areas where she needs to improve. She goes over her notes and reminds herself to keep an eye on the things she has written down because improvements do not happen on their own; you have to be intentional and remind yourself where you trip and where you need to pay close attention next time.

Just like Serena, I have a match book where I write down my goals, areas I need to improve, and things I need to remember to perform better every time.

Here is my process for tracking my goals:

1. Keep a journal where I jot down my top goals.
2. Make daily notes about what must change and what new habits I need to meet my goals.

3. Assess regularly: What worked and what is not working?

4. Review the notes often. (E.g., What were the big epiphanies from last quarter? What did I learn from the feedback conversation that went south? What do I need to remember for next time?)

5. Keep the goal top of mind as I play the game of life and make adjustments. (E.g., Go to bed early to maintain focus during an important meeting tomorrow, don't have difficult conversations at the end of the day when I am tired.)

You not only have to dream big, but you must also be intentional about your goals if you are to achieve them.

Growth Mindset and Taking Risks

Carol Dweck popularized the concept of growth mindset and fixed mindset in her book *Mindset*. Adopting a growth mindset allows you to take risks. A growth mindset is believing that anything can be learned. A fixed mindset is thinking you are born with some talents and skills and you cannot do much to change them. What mindset you want to live by is your choice.

Become aware of your internal dialogue about your ability to learn. A colleague once said to me that she does not have a sticky brain. She meant that she has trouble learning new concepts. Since she accepted that belief about herself, I saw her giving up learning as soon as content got challenging; she did not even try to learn. These beliefs are instilled in us from childhood, either by our parents or our teachers. When they use language like "You will never be good at math" or "You are a bad kid" or even positive phrases like "You are so smart" or "You are genius," they make kids believe that their abilities are predetermined at birth and carved in stone. People with a fixed mindset believe that they have a certain amount of intelligence or certain attributes that cannot be changed or improved. People who adopt a growth mindset believe that, with effort and determination, they can surmount all challenges. This belief in their ability to grow allows them to take more risks. They are not scared of failure.

A few years ago, at a dinner conversation, my brother-in-law made a bold claim that men take more risks than women. Everyone seemed to agree, and I felt very uneasy about that statement. Was it true? In my life experience, I have been a risk-taker, especially in comparison to the men in my life. Was I an exception? When I challenged that statement, everyone took out their phones to google any data that could support or dismiss their own opinions.

Even if it is true that men take more risks than women, I became curious: Are men genetically predisposed to more risk-taking, or are they conditioned that way?

At the playground, I notice the difference in how people parent girls and boys. When a boy falls, they say things like "It was nothing" and "Get back up," while when a girl falls, they sweep her up and give her a big hug, asking her if she is all right. I noticed how protective parents were toward their girls. If, throughout the life of a young girl, everyone is protecting her every move, and when she goes on to school, everyone continues to tolerate boys pushing the boundaries more than girls, isn't it only natural that then boys then turn into adults who are more comfortable taking risks? Of course, this is a gross generalization, and there is massive variation in parenting styles.

After a thorough search, I found no conclusive evidence that supports the claim that boys are genetically predisposed to take bigger risks than girls or that they take more risks. However, there is plenty of research to show that parents treat their sons and daughters differently and are more protective toward their daughters.[18] That and other environmental influences, like boys being exposed to more competitive sports, results in boys building confidence early and taking more risks. Boys get more exposure to not only wins but losses. They learn to take criticism, and they learn to work diligently toward improving themselves. All of these are great growth-mindset qualities to have when entering professional life, and we women can learn to adopt them too.

We must get comfortable taking risks because doing so is essential if we wish to have successful and fulfilling careers.

---

18   Anil Ananthaswamy and Kate Douglas, "How Protective Parents Exacerbate Gender Differences," New Scientist, April 18, 2018, *https://www.newscientist. com/article/mg23831740-700-how-protective-parents-exacerbate-gender-differences/*.

Taking risks means being able to accept failure as an outcome. Sallie Krawcheck, founder of Ellevest, is an inspiring example of a risk-taker and a role model for women who continues to challenge the status quo. She says:

> You have to recognize that success and failure are simply two sides of the same coin: You can't succeed without taking risks. And it's pretty hard to take risks without failing at some point along the way. I know a thing or two about taking career risks: I launched Ellevest the day before the 2016 election and after running several large Wall Street businesses. So there's been success: The chances of Ellevest getting from concept to post-Series-B raise have been calculated at 0.000019%. And there's been a failure: Back in my Wall Street days, I got fired on the front page of The Wall Street Journal . . . twice.
>
> My philosophy is this: If you want to have a big career and you're not making some real mistakes along the way—faceplant stuff—you aren't taking enough risks.
>
> Even in the day-to-day, it's worth acknowledging that with the pace of change in the modern workforce, even trying to avoid risk may be risky. So learn voraciously. Speak up. Stand your ground. Change your mind. Ask the tough question. Nothing happens otherwise.[19]

---

19 Sallie Krawcheck, "3 Pieces of Career Advice You Won't Hear Anywhere Else," Ellevest, August 9, 2022, *https://www.ellevest.com/magazine/career/sallie-krawcheck-top-career-advice/*.

It is not finding your passion that you need to be obsessing about. Instead, get obsessively passionate about learning and taking risks. This is important not only early in your career but throughout your career and life. Once you get passionate about learning, life becomes more meaningful. Not only will you find more joy and fulfillment in what you do, but you will be growing and moving closer to your goal. Learning is exciting when you have a growth mindset. When you believe in your ability to do and learn hard things, your body will crave the adrenaline from the feeling of mastery, the sense of accomplishment from doing something challenging that will further reinforce your confidence in your ability to learn and master hard stuff.

In this chapter, I focused on how to build your competence through a learning mindset. Next, we dive into confidence—because it turns out that confidence is as important as competence in determining success.

Let's dive in!

Chapter 6:
The Power of Confidence

The first time I met Sara, I was in awe of her eloquence. I complimented her on being so beautifully articulate, and she mentioned that she loved public speaking but that, every time she gave a presentation, she broke into a sweat.

Sara was laser-focused on her vision and goals in life. In her teenage years, she had been continuously teased by her brother for being Ms. Goody Two-Shoes and acing her exams. So she learned to walk a fine line: be good but not too good. In her late twenties, she moved back to the city where her family lives so she could get help raising her daughter as a single mom while building a career. For the next fourteen years, her goal was to do well financially to provide for her daughter, Alex. She did well, climbed the echelons of corporate, and gave her daughter the life she had envisioned. One day, she woke up with a realization that Alex was going to college soon. For the past fourteen years, her entire purpose in life had been to obtain financial stability, to provide for her daughter. She had that now. Now what? What was going to be her purpose going forward?

I could see that Sara was at a precipice. Liberated from the burden of her financial obligations, she could imagine new possibilities for her career and dream bigger. She could afford to take more risks toward a more fulfilling and rewarding career.

The only thing she was lacking was that rock-solid confidence in herself, that unwavering belief that she was capable of doing anything she set her mind to, like she had in the past decade, accomplishing her professional goals and giving her tiny family way more than she had set out to.

How does someone like Sara build self-confidence and deal with the subconscious response of panic when she is doing what she loves the most, public speaking? Let me break it down in this chapter.

Confidence is the single most important trait that will speed up your career, make it more joyful and fun, and help you achieve your goals faster. I vehemently believe that confidence matters as much as competence for your career progression.

We are told that if we keep our heads down and work hard, our work will be rewarded and recognized. Today, women earn more college and graduate degrees than men, yet sixty years since women first entered boardrooms, our career trajectories still look very different from men's. Men are still getting promoted and paid more than women. Women face a lot more headwinds because we tend to lead differently, behave differently, and have different needs. While there are big changes needed on the system level, one thing we can take more responsibility for is our confidence. Appearing less confident than men to do the same job where we are equally qualified is holding us back. Let's change that.

My Own Confidence Roller Coaster

The day had come for me to present my dissertation for my master's program. Everything was prepared to a T, the slides and the corresponding script memorized. I looked at the encouraging smiles from my friends and family in the audience, eagerly waiting for my groundbreaking performance.

I nervously stepped onto stage . . . and froze. As I got started, I was sweating profusely, my voice was breaking, my legs were shaking, and I was too afraid to look up from my notes. I had built up so much pressure for this to be perfect that I wanted to blow everyone away with my presentation on carbon sequestration.

I kept going. The first five minutes were nerve-racking. Gradually, though, I shook off the tension, looked up at the audience . . . and began to rely less on my notes.

No one in the room knew the details of CO_2 leaking into an underground aquifer as much as I did. Why was I so afraid? My reptilian brain had kicked in. My reputation was on the line. This was my chance to show everyone how unbelievably awesome I was on stage. But I was not awesome. The pressure I had put on myself crippled my performance.

Looking back on most of my presentations early on in my career, I overprepared, scripted my lines, and generally underdelivered. I was too nervous and simply was not confident in my ability to present and explain the topic, and therefore I struggled to make the impact I desired. I knew the content really well, but if I was not able to explain it with confidence, I was not able to get across my knowledge on the topic effectively. My lack of confidence early in my career hurt my progress. I was taken less seriously, I was seen as someone who did not know enough to take on more responsibility, and I was left to do easier, more repetitive tasks for far too long.

I was a confident kid growing up. I loved being on stage, participating in speech and debate contests when I was as young as seven years old. Somewhere down the line, into adolescence and beyond, that confidence withered. I became self-conscious and aware of the world and others around me who were better than me. I moved to the US, a nation known for its exuberant confidence (or overconfidence!), at the age of eighteen. My English was good but not in comparison to the natives. I did not have the same fluidity, the same ability to articulate and express myself in a second language. My public speaking confidence faltered even further.

A lot has happened since my frailing moment presenting my dissertation. The version of me who stands on stage today is full of confidence when she presents to a crowd of a thousand. I have spent fourteen years perfecting the art of public speaking, taking advantage of every opportunity I could to speak in front of crowds. I joined a local Toastmasters group and pushed myself into uncomfortable speaking situations. I raised my hand to speak at weddings, speaking impromptu; I volunteered to be a host at a women's conference and prepared diligently to give my best performance. The more I appeared on stage, the more comfortable I got, to the point that it became easy for me to say yes when asked at the last minute to be on the stage at an event with over a thousand attendees. Today, my confidence has grown, and I regularly speak in front of large audiences. This confidence spills over to my job and opens doors to more exciting roles and board positions.

Confidence and Competence

The human brain mistakes confidence for competence. Even if you are competent in your subject matter, if you are unable to present with confidence, people will question your competence. People hire confident candidates because they mistake high confidence for competence when the two do not always correlate.

Competence is how good you are at something. Confidence is how good you think you are at something. Competence can help boost your confidence, but simply increasing your confidence will not make you more competent.

Women often display less confidence and are therefore perceived as less competent, which is why, in a hiring situation, male candidates get an advantage even if their actual competence may be less than that of their female colleagues. They displayed more confidence!

Being Confident Does Not Mean You Cannot Be Humble

Contrary to what some think, confidence and humility are not opposites. You can present your work with confidence and be open to being challenged. Being humble allows us to double-check our answers and be open to the possibility that we may be wrong.

When someone can admit they are wrong, that displays immense self-confidence. It shows that they are able to listen deeply to those who disagree, consider their arguments, and change their mind. That kind of intellectual maturity is hard to find in our rigid corporate cultures. As a leader, I have found myself arguing my point of view simply for the sake of winning arguments. I was afraid to be wrong, thinking it would make me look foolish as a leader. But then I saw that some more revered leaders were never afraid to be wrong. Steve Jobs famously said, "I do not care about being right. I care about success and doing the right thing."

My job is to get it right. It's not to personally be right myself. I changed my approach and, instead of trying hard to keep my stance, I try to lose arguments. I seek points of view that oppose my own. I realized that this garnered me way more respect and influence as a leader than trying to prove myself right ever did.

So how can you get started with building your self-confidence?

Five Steps to Building Your Confidence

1. Decide What You Want to Become Confident At

Here is the thing: you do not have to be confident at everything. I am confident speaking to a crowd, approaching new people, and asking difficult questions, but there are plenty of things that I am not confident in, such as parallel parking, downhill skiing, and mental math. In areas where I am confident, I have deliberately decided to become more confident and worked on it diligently: public speaking, building innovation teams, and facilitating workshops. I may not always be skillful and amazing every time, but I go in there with confidence. When I am confident in my ability to figure things out, it makes a world of a difference in the experience and the outcome. I do not get nervous because I have reframed that feeling in my stomach as excitement right before going on stage. I am bubbling with excitement!

Get to know yourself. We all have some inherent superpowers within us—our talents, our abilities, things that come a lot easier to us than they do to other people. What are your inherent strengths? To learn more about your unique abilities, you can ask the people closest to you what they see as your strengths, or you can take the Gallup StrengthsFinder/ CliftonStrengths test to get some insights.

For example, if you are really good at complex engineering analysis, great. Get even better at it and be confident in your work. Solve harder and harder problems, and eventually your confidence will grow. As you build your confidence in one area, it will propel you forward in other areas as you build self-esteem and self-confidence. If you understand a specific engineering concept better than others, talk about it—with confidence. Get noticed, and be comfortable with the attention.

Use your inherent strengths to advance your purpose in life. Use your intrinsic motivations to enhance your confidence. If you are motivated to teach people and share your knowledge, put yourself in situations where you do more of that so that you start building your confidence. It is easier to keep on working on something that is driven by intrinsic motivations.

2. Other People's Judgment Does Not Define You

I had been in my leadership role for two months when one of the more experienced men on my team came up to me in an attempt to show solidarity. "Nada, do you know that there are many people who are surprised that you got this role? People are talking about you in the hallway, saying that you are inexperienced, not qualified. But I just want to say that I think it's amazing that you got this job. I have worked with you, so I know you. You have my full support."

Whether he meant it or not, this man was spreading gossip or couching subtle insults in an alleged compliment. I smiled at him and deliberately did not indulge in that conversation. Nada from a few years ago would have asked, "Who are these people? What are they saying?" I would have fallen right into the trap. I would have let that one comment destroy my confidence. I would have ruminated over it for days. It is in this type of situation where your confidence in yourself needs to be rock-solid.

Such comments are at best just plain clumsiness or, at worst, an intimidation tactic. Either way, they can activate the insecure side of you, causing you to begin to doubt yourself. I do not want to be cynical and imply that you cannot trust people, but you cannot control what people say about you behind your back. People can act in sleazy ways. It does not make them bad people; they just react to situations in an instinctive way when they feel threatened. They get engulfed in feelings of envy and use their words to bring the threat down.

As a leader, I try to be forgiving and give people the benefit of doubt. Perhaps this man meant to make me feel insecure, or perhaps that was not his intention at all. I can choose the reality I want to believe in. Which reality would help me lead from a place of love and compassion for my team?

I love this saying from Simon Sinek: "If you want to achieve anything in this world, you have to get used to the idea that not everyone will like you[20]."

I built my self-confidence by putting myself out there over and over again and exposing myself to judgment. Especially

---

20   Simon Sinek (@simonsinek), "If you want to achieve anything in this world, you have to get used to the idea that not everyone will like you," Twitter, January 18, 2013, 9:08 a.m., https://twitter.com/simonsinek/status/292302362708680704.

in the age of social media, I know that I will be judged one hundred times over. Not everyone will like what I have to say, and that is okay.

I keep this Teddy Roosevelt quote with me, on my desk or in my notebook, and I read it every time I am faced with scathing criticism:

> It is not the critic who counts; not the man who points out how the strong [woman] stumbles or where the doer of deeds could have done them better. The credit belongs to the [woman] who is actually in the arena, whose face is marred by dust and sweat and blood; who strives valiantly; who errs, who comes short again and again, because there is no effort without error and shortcoming; but who does actually strive to do the deeds; who knows great enthusiasms, the great devotions; who spends [herself] in a worthy cause; who at the best knows in the end the triumph of high achievement, and who at the worst, if [she] fails, at least fails while daring greatly, so that [her] place shall never be with those cold and timid souls who neither know victory nor defeat.[21]

---

21   Theodore Roosevelt (1910), "Citizenship in a Republic," Transcript of speech delivered at the Sorbonne, Paris, France, April 23, 1910, https://www.presidency.ucsb.edu/documents/address-the-sorbonne-paris-france-citizenship-republic.

It is not the critic who counts; it is you, the person who is in the arena. The person who is taking action on their visions and dreams. When you put yourself out there, people will judge. Period. It will happen. You cannot control other people's thoughts. You can only control your own.

This is easier said than done. Here are some ways that I have worked with myself over the years to let the criticism roll off my back easily.

- Keep a compliments diary. Every time someone gives you a specific compliment on something you have done, note it down. Come back to it whenever you need a lift. Over the years, this will become a long list of reminders of what you are good at and how most people think about you.

- Stop yourself from seeking incessant validation. Early on in my career, whenever I gave a presentation, I would go around asking people for feedback and validation. Was the presentation good? Did I do okay? I was fishing for compliments because I felt insecure inside. Once I realized that I was doing this to feel better about myself, I began to stop. I do not need constant validation about my performance from others. I am my own judge. Instead, I should seek feedback from select people who I truly respect and believe will add value. (More on this in chapter 13, "Feedback Culture.")

- When you do receive criticism, ask what the person's motive or intention was for delivering that criticism. Often, criticism has nothing to do with you and more to do with the person giving it. Most people who are criticizing and not trying to lift you up want to bring you down to feel better about themselves.
- Do not take everything personally. Remember, our goal is not perfection. Our goal is to get better and to learn.

3. Do Not Let Childhood Insecurities Hurt Your Adult Confidence

When I was in sixth grade, a new girl came to our school. She became immediately popular with me and many of my friends. Over time, she told them stories about me that made them not want to be my friend. I felt really frustrated, as there was nothing I could do about this. She was telling other girls that I lied, that I borrowed a book from her and returned it in bad shape, that I was a mean person. I felt ashamed. I knew that the rumors were not true but I could not do anything to prove her wrong. Over time, my friends chose this girl over me, and by the end of middle school, I felt shunned by my friends.

Over the span of those two years my confidence crumbled. For the first time, I became exposed to how fragile one's reputation is, how anyone can say anything about you and people will believe them. I decided to retreat, to not be so visible and to put my head in the books.

As I grew older, I feared that the same story was repeating itself. I picked up on signals that made me feel that the world was conspiring against me, that people were talking behind my back. The trauma from when I was twelve years old was resurfacing every time I found myself in a situation where I was criticized. I would easily become paranoid that others would think I was an impostor.

It is very typical for adults to carry such childhood traumas with them into adulthood. (And to be clear, when I use the word *trauma*, in no way do I mean to undermine devastating monumental events that some children and adults go through that have severe debilitating impact on their life.)

All of us experienced some form of micro-traumas growing up. In psychology, the word *micro-trauma* is used to define even seemingly minor, subtle events that lead to a lasting impact on us as adults. Unless we work to resolve our childhood traumas, we continue to live at their mercy.

For me, it was through my own personal reflection that I became aware of my triggers and what circumstances made me feel paranoid. Was I triggered based on my childhood experience, or was there a real cause for concern? I realized that when my insecurities kicked in, I was seeing the world through the eyes of a twelve-year-old girl, not through my modern reality.

I realized that everything was not about me. I was not the center of everyone else's universe. The world was not conspiring against me. Even if I was criticized, it did not mean that I could not change the minds of those criticizing me, or that they were going around talking to other people behind my back. I realized that my childhood insecurities were hurting my adult confidence. Once I faced those insecurities, I was able to go through life with renewed confidence. I stopped making criticism bigger than just words from one person. it was *not* a reflection of the broader view of society. It did not define me.

4. Have Courage and Confidence Will Follow

The secret to confidence is courage: courage to risk failure. It takes courage to show up when your confidence is frail. But if you show up every single day, confidence will almost always follow.

When I am faced with something difficult, I remind myself that I am building my confidence muscle. I am in training. The more hard things I do, the easier they get, and I become more confident in my ability. Just like driving a car or riding a bike, we are all scared the first couple of times, but when we do something repeatedly, our stress levels decline, we build confidence in our ability, and we can leave it to our subconscious. Our bodies know what to do.

Public speaking is no different. Personally, I made a point to give a speech or present almost every day. At work, you will have many opportunities to present. It could be something as simple as presenting the agenda for a meeting.

Think about what you wanted to become more confident at. What's one thing you can do every day to start building that confidence? Decide on one small action you can take toward that goal, and have the courage to take it.

Know that the more you show up with courage, the more confidence will follow.

5. Raise Your Hand

One action you can take to start building your confidence is raising your hand. The more you raise your hand in meetings, at conferences, and at events, the less intimidating it gets and the more you get used to the attention on you.

Early in my career, during one of our strategy meetings, my boss was telling everyone about a new strategy and how we were going to get there. He was not looking for anyone's input, and it was not a discussion. Finally, toward the end of the day, he asked what we could do to get to our goals. No one raised their hands. The whole day had gone by, and it had just been him telling us how he thought everything was going to play out and what we were going to do. When he finally asked for input, nobody raised their hands. People did not feel that they could contribute.

I decided to raise my hand and bring up the elephant in the room. I told him, "If we are to achieve our goals, we also have to work on our culture. We must allow people to speak up and express their views without striking them down right away."

The entire room looked at me in awe. I had dared to speak up. But most importantly, my boss came up to me later and thanked me for speaking up. He noticed me, and he decided to charge me with the responsibility of executing the new strategy. It was a wonderful opportunity that I would not have received had I not raised my hand.

As soon as I showed up with a fearless attitude toward the world, I was awarded more respect, and more opportunities presented themselves. I was being noticed. Confidence allowed me to fully express myself and not hold back my desires and ambitions. When I showed up with my strong side, my strengths propelled me forward. Not only was I getting more opportunities, I was enjoying my work more, and I was showing up as the best version of myself. I was showing up unhindered by other people's judgments and expectations.

Go get 'em!

Chapter 7:

Labels You Carry with You

You are *what* you are, you are *where* you are, and you are *who* you are because of what you believe about yourself. Your beliefs are the thoughts you keep consciously or unconsciously accepting as the law in your life. Whether you are aware of them or not, they still affect your reality.

— *Joe Dispenza*

Sheryl Sandberg told me to lean in. And so I did. I raised my hand, I applied for that job, I let it be known that I wanted more.

I went up to the head of HR. I shared with her what I wanted in my career, that I wanted to play an important role in growing my company and achieving its goals. I shared my leadership ambitions and told her that I wanted to ensure that I got on that track with her support and guidance. I asked her what it was going to take. What opportunities were available?

She looked at me with a blank stare and said, "I see you are ambitious. You need to be patient."

That was it.

She didn't say, "That's great, let me help you." She just said, "I see you are ambitious." Her message to me was that if I was patient and did good work, opportunities would appear. "Believe in magic," she was telling me.

I felt quite vulnerable having revealed my ambitions, and I left her office with the feeling that I had done something wrong.

A few days later, I found myself repeating to myself, "I am an ambitious woman, and there is nothing wrong with that." Why did I feel the need to say that? Did I need to convince myself that ambition was not a bad thing? As a child, as a young girl, the message I had gotten was "Work hard, shine bright, but don't talk too much about it. Have ambitions but don't talk about it. Talking about it will expose you to the evil eye, and you are more prone to bad luck if you reveal your dreams and desires." As I grew older, society gave me subtle nudges to be more modest, more self-effacing, and less assertive. It was a great recipe to be more likable. We teach girls to make themselves small, to shrink themselves, and to not have too much ambition.

So then, when the likes of Sheryl Sandberg told me to lean in, to take charge, I definitely had some societal conditioning to overcome to fully embrace ambition and be less discreet about it. It did not help that, early on in my career, I had landed a job that took me to Scandinavia. There is social code in the Nordics known as the *janteloven*—the law of Jante. In practice, it translates to "Don't think you are better than anyone else. Don't be that poppy seed that hoovers over the others. Be humble. Don't boast. Don't brag."

Scandinavian society is built around generous ideals of collectiveness, with an altruistic focus on what we can achieve together as a society by putting the community before the individual. Collectiveness is a powerful concept that has given way to a robust social welfare model where citizens get equal access to health care, education, childcare, and unemployment benefits.

However, on the individual level, it can be stifling. It is harder to motivate and encourage individuals to live a better life and pursue their dreams if they are to suppress their unique talents. Of course, I see plenty of ambition in the Nordics, but artifacts of "let us all be average" mindset remain, particularly impacting women. Perhaps that is what the head of HR saw: someone who was too individualistic, who wanted to stand out, who thought she was better than her colleagues.

Working in male-dominated environments, however, has exposed me to sufficient ambition to know that in men ambition is normal, it is *needed*, to succeed, and it gets them far. In one of my business trips to my company's office in Florida, I was impressed by the sheer honesty of the head of the country office. He was very comfortable in sharing with everyone that he had applied for the head of region position. In men, ambition and drive are not weaknesses but strengths. In women, these traits can be perceived as aggression and egoism. In 2020, a global survey showed that women are hesitant to actually call themselves or be labeled ambitious— it doesn't have a positive connotation for women.[22]

To overcome this societal conditioning, I sought mentors who were unapologetically ambitious. I learned from them, and having them around normalized ambition for me. My drive is an integral part of who I am. It's been with me my whole life.

They say that when you're a second child, you grow up craving attention. I had a sister who was only a year and a half older than me. However, my sister was loving and empathetic from a very young age. She watched over me, she fed me, and she came to my defense when I got in trouble. She would unselfishly let me take the limelight (and she still does). For the most part, she did not have to do much, as I got myself in enough trouble to be the center of attention. I was outspoken, even as a kid. I spoke up when I thought I or my siblings were treated unfairly. When all the cousins at my grandparents' multigenerational house where we all lived would band together and tell us we were not allowed to play with them,

---

22 Marguerite Ward, "Women Are Afraid to Call Themselves 'Ambitious' at Work and It's Seriously Hurting Their Careers," Insider, March 8, 2020, *https://www.businessinsider.com/psychologist-recommend-strategies-ambition-women-at-work-career-goals*.

I asked for what I wanted. I took the lead. My grandmother called me *hurri mirich* (green chili), which I think meant that I was hot-headed, I was clever, and I could jump at you at any moment. I did not like being called that, but I get why she would call me that.

As a child, I became aware that people perceive me as *chalak*, the Urdu word for *clever*. It somehow had a negative connotation, perhaps because the word can also mean *conniving*. It wasn't that I had ill intentions, but I was strategic. I was always two steps ahead.

My grandfather lived on the first floor of our two-story house. His room had a huge steel cupboard that was always locked. It was not a cabinet, but rather a huge cupboard where he kept all his precious belongings, including his handgun and all his cash. This is also where he kept candy for his grandkids who lived in the house. Every few days, we would go up to him and ask him if we could have some. He had three different types, and everyone could only get one of each. One day, I went down to ask if I could collect candy for all the kids in the house. He gave me three of each candy for each of the six kids in the house. I could barely carry it all in my two hands. I climbed up the stairs to my parents' room and chucked it all under the bed in a baby bassinet that was lying there. I am not sure if I intended to give everyone their share at some point—I just know that I didn't. I would go and help myself to a candy every few days. It lasted me a while.

My parents tell the story of my grandfather finding me sitting on the steps, eating the candy. I don't have a recollection of that memory, but that means that I did this more than once. My grandfather was a stern man, but he did not get angry; he just laughed and told everyone the story. I was a bit ashamed, but I was never punished. He continued to trust me.

My grandfather's continued faith taught me that I could be trusted, that I was capable of doing the right thing despite my past infractions. I did not need to be punished; I needed someone who could see the good in me, who would continue to trust me so I could find it in myself to become a better person.

We grow up with many labels, but having even one person show you that they believe in you can change your entire trajectory.

One of my fellow board members at one of my companies told me a story that illustrates this. He serves on many boards and has had a very successful career as a CEO and executive leader, but he told me that he was a troubled kid and did not do well in school. After high school, he decided to join the police force. There, he had one manager who took him under his wing and said, "You are a smart kid. You are meant for bigger things. You should go back to school." He remembers that as a defining moment, as it was the first time that someone truly saw him and said that they believed in him.

He ended up going to law school, acing it, and being CEO of one of the biggest companies in Norway. He defied all the labels, just because one person believed in him.

The influence of such people on an individual is remarkable even in adulthood. Leaders, mentors, coaches and teachers have a huge responsibility, they can make or break a person with their belief or with their labels.

Labels instill in us limiting beliefs about who we are and what we are capable of. They hold us back from expressing ourselves fully so that we can achieve our most desired goals.

So what are the limiting beliefs that have held me back that you can learn from on your career journey?

Chapter 8:

Limiting Beliefs

Our deepest fear is not that we are inadequate.
Our deepest fear is that we are powerful beyond measure.
It is our light, not our darkness, that most frightens us.
We ask ourselves, "Who am I to be brilliant, gorgeous, talented, fabulous?"
Actually, who are you not to be?

— *Marianne Williamson*

When I told people that I had quit my job, I got two types of responses.

There were people who said, "Wow, what a risky move, leaving when you are at the top. Aren't you afraid you won't be able to come back at the same level?"

And there were people who said, "Wow, you had clearly outgrown where you were. There are so many opportunities. What are you going to do next?"

These two points of view represent very different ways of viewing the world. One sees the situation as an opportunity, and the other sees it as a threat. Our perspective all comes down to the inner narrative within ourselves. Those who respond with fear are carrying beliefs that limit their view of possibilities, while those who respond with optimism have beliefs that guide them toward endless possibilities.

Limiting beliefs are thoughts, opinions, and stories that we tell ourselves about who we are and what we are capable of and that hold us back from truly creating our best lives and becoming who we are meant to be. They often appear in the form of self-deprecating thoughts that we repeat to ourselves: *I cannot do this, I am not smart enough, my brain does not work like that, I am not focused enough, I am not knowledgeable enough.*

These beliefs lie in our subconsciousness, often originating from childhood or early adulthood, influencing the decisions we make and, to a great extent, impacting our careers in a negative way. They are an evolutionary response to keep you safe, but they prevent you from stepping up and taking risks because they cause you to fear failure or humiliation. These beliefs are like blinders, preventing us from seeing the full scope of possibility; instead, we continue seeing the world through our limited vision and beliefs.

You want to become aware of these beliefs so that you can replace them with more empowering alternatives. In this chapter, I shed light on some of the most prevalent limiting beliefs I have had, limiting beliefs that I overcame and that you can too.

Limiting Belief #1: You Shouldn't Be Too Ambitious

In the last chapter, I talked extensively about being ambitious and about how, for many, the word *ambition* can have a negative connotation. The idea that we can be too ambitious is a limiting belief that we develop when we are young girls, influenced by the subtle messages we get from society. Sheryl Sandberg made us aware that using the term *bossy* for young girls when they take charge and demonstrate leadership skills can have negative impacts.

When we realize that we are not liked for being confident and for winning, we start playing small. We learn to sacrifice our own desires and ambitions for society's benefit.

We all want to be viewed as humble, so we make our ambitions small. But being ambitious and being humble are not opposites; they can coexist. So all you women who have a fire in your bellies, do not repress it. Give it space. You are not meant to shrink your ambition.

Limiting Belief #2: It's Best to Stay Grounded and Be Realistic

I have always been a dreamer. Dreaming allowed me to think beyond what was realistically possible. As I grew older, the world told me to be realistic. I learned that you create your own reality. What is realistic for one person may be completely unrealistic for another. It is only up to you to decide what is a reality for you.

For many young girls in Pakistan, it would have been unrealistic to think that it would be possible to go study abroad at sixteen. I did not let other people's limiting beliefs stop me from trying. I created my own reality. I found a way to make my dream come true. Instead of believing that you have to stay grounded, replace this belief with the more empowering belief that you live in a universe of endless possibility and that you can invent your own reality.

Limiting Belief #3: I Am Not Ready Yet

Early in my career, I remember passing on so many opportunities because I did not think that I was ready. I only applied for jobs where I knew I was qualified. It is normal to think that way early in your career. But I have also seen people who believe that they are ready before they really are. They are able to move up faster, they expose themselves to more opportunities, and they do not pre-decide that they are not qualified. Information and knowledge are infinite, and sometimes we can get stuck in a learning trap, thinking we need to know more, learn more, and gain more experience. At some point, you also have to start applying the learning, start producing and executing on all the knowledge. That does not mean that you stop learning, because you will always learn more by practicing. The only way to know for sure when you are ready is when you have tried it, when you have attempted it.

If you are part of a project where you are doing all the analysis but haven't dared to present to the client yet, just try it, and you will figure out if you are ready or not. Most of the time, you will realize that you were more than ready! This mindset is particularly applicable when we pass on leadership opportunities thinking, *I do not have enough experience and everyone in my team is ten years older than me.* You may be the only one who has leadership skills, and unless you raise your hand and have a go at the opportunities available to you, you and others have no way of knowing.

Limiting Belief #4: There Is Only One Path

This is one of the most common limiting beliefs: believing that how others progress or achieve their goals is the only way. There are many ways to achieve your goals, and you have to define your own path. Your path may be completely different from others' paths; in fact, it most likely will be. You may be the first person to be the CEO of an engineering company who does not have an engineering degree and is of a different gender. Your path to that CEO role will most likely be different from your predecessors' paths, but it comes down to believing that you can still arrive at the same destination.

So create your own path that is tailored to who you are. Trust that there are many ways of achieving your goals, and if one path did not lead you where you wanted to go, there will be others.

Remember, you have to enjoy the journey to the destination, and the best way to do that is to be who you are and to do what you love to do.

Become aware of these limiting beliefs and challenge yourself to believe the opposite of each one. Here are potential reframes.

1. Reframe "You shouldn't be too ambitious" to "Pursuing my ambitions is the best thing for myself and the world."
2. Reframe "It's best to stay grounded and be realistic" to "When I believe in my dreams, they become my reality."
3. Reframe "I am not ready yet" to "I have been preparing for this all my life. I am as ready as I can be."
4. Reframe "There is only one path" to "I create my own path to success that is meaningful and joyful for me."

Make these opposite statements your affirmations and repeat them to yourself daily.

But remember, this will have no impact if you do not believe in these reframes, so here is an exercise you can do when you have some time to reflect:

1. Spend some time with each one of these limiting beliefs and ponder how you may be limiting yourself through such thinking.

2. In this process, you may encounter limiting beliefs beyond those I listed above. Write them down on a piece of paper.
3. Ask yourself where each belief originates from. Try to identify the situations or people who perpetuate this belief in you. You may have adopted the belief as a protective mechanism, but it is not serving you anymore.
4. Next to each belief, write down how it has a damaging impact on your career and your life in general.
5. Write down what the opposite of each belief would look like. Make that your affirmation, and remind yourself of this new belief daily until it becomes part of your subconscious.

When your mind and body finally understand that it is a good thing for the world that you are ambitious, you will feel a surge of energy, and you will take action toward your goals. When you write your goals down, you will not force yourself to play small. The goals will excite you. You will subdue the voice that says, "This is not realistic." You will tell yourself, "This is my reality. I am ready for this, and this is my own unique journey."

When you start uprooting these deeply held beliefs (that have often been embedded in you since childhood), you will begin to build a career that is meaningful and deeply fulfilling to you. You will stop doubting yourself and truly start believing in your abilities. You will find purpose, and it will become much harder to hold yourself back.

Chapter 9:

Diversity, Equity, and Inclusion

Society: Be different.
Society: Not like that.

— Unknown

When Sofie entered the meeting room, she caught everyone's attention. She embodied this immense energy that you sensed right away. She was lively and free-spirited. She expressed herself fully, in her demeanor, in her impeccable taste in clothes, and through her smile and laughter. She was an outlier in the engineering firm where we both worked.

First of all, being a woman you are automatically an outlier, but you could tell Sofie's mind just worked differently. Instead of bringing a notepad with an engineering grid, she would bring a large notepad made for artists with big blank pages, and she carefully placed five colorful pens in neat order next to what seemed like a canvas. As each meeting progressed, she would draw a beautiful mind map. She was unconventional. It did not take her long to get into the technical details of the new scrubber technology we were evaluating for ships. Sofie had a PhD in chemistry; she knew her stuff.

She was one of the few young talents to get a special invite to the yearly strategy meeting for all the leaders in the maritime business unit. Being one of the few women in a sea of men with black suits, she decided to assert herself, to be unconventional, so she started her presentation with a five-minute meditation. The leaders loved it! They loved her ability to break from the norm and bring a different energy onstage. They admired her confidence in daring to do things differently.

As she was promoted through the ranks of management, though, that same confidence and diversity that had been so admired became her Achilles' heel. Those traits that were so valued when she was in less prestigious roles were no longer valued as she got more experienced and entered influential meeting rooms. "You do not have executive presence," she was told. "You do not fit the mold. You are too disruptive."

She ended up with a boss who really did not see what made her special. She was mistreated and undermined repeatedly. I met up with her for coffee a few years after our first interaction, and I was shocked to see how she had changed. She had shriveled like a leaf, no longer connected to the source of inspiration inside her. Her energy had been sapped by the continuous battle between who she was and what the company, her manager, wanted her to be.

Sadly, I have seen this story repeated over and over again. We admire difference from afar, but we struggle to devise systems to include those who do not fit the norm.

As a leader, you are not only responsible for ensuring diversity, but you are also responsible for ensuring a culture where diversity can thrive. Diversity is not simply defined in terms of protected classes—age, race, gender, or orientation. Equally important is neurodiversity: people who are able to think and behave differently and who have different opinions, life experiences, and perspectives. The best-performing team is not the one that is made up of the intellectually smartest people in a room; instead, it's a cross-functional team with complementary skills and multidisciplinary knowledge. Diversity is about having dissenting voices that push us to think again and check our blind spots and not fall prey to groupthink mentality.

Having diverse candidates alone is not enough. You need to create a culture of inclusion to ensure that these diverse candidates can function effectively, so that they collaborate and take advantage of the experience and skills in the room. As a leader, you create the culture. You create psychological safety so everyone feels safe to speak and contribute with their skills, knowledge, expertise, and points of view. Psychological safety means that people are not afraid to show up as their authentic selves, be vulnerable, and challenge the status quo. Psychological safety is essential for innovative thinking, which is imperative in today's rapidly changing environment, at the individual, team, and organizational levels.[23]

Conformity

As an agile leader, you trust your team to do their work to the best of the ability. You are an inclusive leader and respect people for their individuality and the unique strengths they bring in. You are not expecting them to conform to certain stereotypes.

Pressures to conform work against psychological safety and against our diversity, equity, and inclusion (DEI) goals. We create a conformity culture because we believe that if everyone adheres to certain norms, it makes it easier to maintain power and control a big organization. We use terms like *cultural fit* as a code for a person's ability to conform to a culture of long working hours, ruthless feedback, competitiveness, and things like dress code. Unfortunately, if we are sticklers for conformity, we compromise on diversity, equity, and inclusion. Where is the diversity if everyone is expected to act, behave, and think the same way?

Gary Hamel and Michele Zanini write about the history of bureaucratic organization in their book *Humanocracy: Creating Organizations as Amazing as the People Inside*

---

23 Amy C. Edmondson, *The Fearless Organization: Creating Psychological Safety in the Workplace for Learning, Innovation, and Growth* (Hoboken, NJ: John Wiley & Sons, 2018).

Them. Bureaucracy is deep-seated in most corporate cultures, "with its authoritarian power structures, suffocating rules, and toxic politicking."[24]

Our corporate cultures have been devised and evolved over the past 200 years to maximize conformity. Hamel and Zanini propose an alternative, *humanocracy*, a system that inspires people to give their best. Instead of focusing on holding on to power, it is about maximizing contribution. Company cultures that can hold real diversity, with minimum pressures to conform, become resilient, creative, and adaptive, giving room to new solutions and innovations.

Isn't conformity essential for consistency and complex coordination in big organizations? In fact, the agile movement has shown that giving teams autonomy leads to better performance, and autonomy allows people devise their own ways of work that suit them. Even outside of avant-garde tech companies, we find example of empowering leadership in companies like the US steelmaker Nucor and the Chinese company Haier, the biggest appliance maker in the world.[25] These companies show that it is possible to have the benefits of bureaucracy, the structure and consistency, without sacrificing the freedom, creativity, and individuality of people in these companies.

---

24 Gary Hamel and Michele Zanini, *Humanocracy: Creating Organizations as Amazing as the People Inside Them* (Boston: Harvard Business Review Press, 2020).

25 Hamel and Zanini.

I do not propose anarchy-style freedom—we need corporate codes of conduct, boundaries on how we operate, clear performance expectations, and company values that employees should adhere to—but we should not penalize or hold biases and judgments against employees who do not conform to the mainstream dominant culture. To allow people to be authentic and bring their selves to work means that we tolerate people's eccentricities and get comfortable with healthy friction. Too often, we use feedback, performance reviews, and training to try to change people so that they all act, behave, and think the same way. We say things like, "They are so smart, but if only they were not so direct" or "If only they displayed better executive presence." When we try to change people, we lose the benefits of diversity. Of course, people can always improve their skills, but that is different from asking people to change who they are at their core. Diversity in people is not a problem to be solved; it is an opportunity and a challenge that we need to manage.

Metrics That Work against Diversity

When I moved on to a new role, my new boss asked for some feedback from my previous manager, Adam, on how I operate. He forwarded that email on to me:

> I hired Nada for the role of head of innovation.
>
> It is important to realize that what I was looking for in this role was somebody who behaved, thought, and was motivated in a different way from most of the rest of the people in the company.

That is exactly what I was looking for and why I hired her.

When we think about what we want for Nada in the future, we should pause to reflect whether we want her to "conform" or whether we want her motivations and focus to be a bit different. Is it possible for her to do both, personally I think yes, it is.

For the future I think it is important to create extremely tangible objectives where the outcome can be measured and the value of the objective visualised. Measuring innovation is hard and there is a risk that Nada risks being seen as "not producing tangible results." Measuring continuous improvement can be extremely tangible.

Adam was aware of the implications of having a nonconformist person in the company and the struggles he and other managers would face managing someone who did not fit the box. He wanted someone with a particular mindset and capabilities in the role. The position was head of innovation, after all, and if the company was going to change the way they did things, they needed new perspectives.

I did well in the role because Adam allowed me to be myself and gave me autonomy. I challenged him to do things differently, and while he did not go along with every new idea, he let me experiment and use my strengths to inspire not only him but the organization as a whole with a new way of working, which was remarkable for an engineering firm that has been operating for over 200 years. I was creative and pushed boundaries on the risks my boss was willing to take. I was performing well, as I had the support to go above and beyond. I was noticed by senior management, and when a new VP of transformation role opened up, I was offered the job. It was perfect for me and completely aligned with my vision for myself and how I wanted to help transform the company to face the future.

Adam also touched on the struggle of measuring innovation with our usual operational metrics, metrics like number of sales, revenue, and costs saved. In fact, operational metrics, when applied to innovation teams, are stifling. I worked closely with Adam to redefine metrics for myself and my team that were more aligned with what we were trying to achieve. The work with Adam—and later with Mario, my new boss—made me realize how uniform metrics across the board may be working against diversity. If everyone is assessed the same way, how will employees be encouraged to do things differently? Setting metrics and KPIs is challenging in itself (I love John Doerr's book *Measure What Matters* on this topic), and if we have to account for diversity, it makes these things more complicated. Yet I believe setting the appropriate metrics requires serious consideration. How are we measuring individuals within a team? Are we assessing them based on their strengths or using general metrics that are the same for everyone? I was lucky in my career to have had managers who asked me what my own career goals were and helped me set metrics that aligned with my strengths, my goals, and the company goals. That way, I was intrinsically motivated to improve and perform well.

I have also had the experience of a boss who felt that, to progress in the company, one had to be like him. It took me a while, unfortunately, to realize that I could not do all the things that I was really good at and also give him what he needed. He measured me on the number of tasks I got done and the number of projects I took on, while, as a people manager, I measured my success on effective leadership and on building a high-performance team that would ultimately take care of execution and achieving our objectives. I felt immense pressure to conform, and I ultimately decided to leave, as I was not able to perform the way the company wanted me to.

When I left, Adam said to me, "Nada, you do not belong here. You are an entrepreneur. Start your own business or find a more innovative company to work for. Find a place where you can be you." Even though I know Adam meant this in a good way, it just shows the prevalent mindset in that organization. It did not create space for diversity. If you did not fit into the norm, you did not belong. You had to be like everybody else in the organization to succeed.

What Adam did not understand is that everyone wants to feel like they belong at their workplace.

Sustaining Diversity

I was having lunch with three software engineers in the company, and they revealed to me that they were all planning to quit. Each of these women had been at the company a year or less, but they were not assigned to interesting tasks, no one was responsible for their development, and they simply felt demotivated. One of them said that because she was not getting to use her creativity at work, she was thinking of going back to school to become an architect. Work is where one should be using their creativity!

I was baffled. Here were three highly competent women with technical master's degrees in a male-dominated environment where we were struggling to increase our diversity numbers. We manage to hire them, but we took no responsibility to onboard them properly and give them the support they needed to succeed and feel like they belong. We were simply not doing enough to make them stay.

When we truly start believing that diversity is good for business, we will work harder to keep these women in the workplace and not put the responsibility on their shoulders to do more to fit in. We need diversity in leadership for effective decision-making, for better problem-solving, and for more empathy and compassion for those we serve.

Diversity also exists within women and men. Some are more analytical, while others lean toward creativity and intuition.

Both types can be phenomenal leaders. It is not just the rational thinkers who are great executors that make awesome leaders, but also those who end up on the other side of whichever personality test you use. What we get wrong is that equality is not about treating everyone the same way. It is about letting everyone be who they are, catering to their differences, and ensuring that they have an equal chance of getting that promotion and raise, despite the fact that they don't all fit the norm.

Women Lead Differently

Women lead differently than men do. Only 8.5 percent of Fortune 500 companies are led by women, yet these companies tend to outperform both in public and private markets and yield higher returns on all fronts. CNBC journalist Julia Boorstin interviewed thousands of CEOs over twenty-plus years as a business journalist and identifies several key characteristics that women leaders displayed that are not traditionally associated with male leaders: vulnerability and gratitude, focus on purpose along with profits, and a communal leadership style. She found that women leaders are not just fitting in—once they make it to the top, they are operating differently from the vast majority of male leaders and are solving problems differently.[26]

---

26 Julia Boorstin, When Women Lead: What They Achieve, Why They Succeed, and How We Can Learn from Them (Avid Reader Press, 2022).

She writes:

> [*I wanted*] to help people see the array of successful leaders that looked nothing like the archetypal tech CEO; the kind who was determined to "move fast and break things" (a quote Mark Zuckerberg famously put on posters at Facebook's first headquarters). These women also looked nothing like the female CEO anti-hero Elizabeth Holmes, whose spectacular failure created a new negative stereotype of female leadership . . . I saw how what seemed to be atypical, seemingly inimitable women leaders could be new, imitable archetypes. And I saw how women, because they already didn't fit the stereotypes of what leaders were supposed to look like, often felt liberated to do things their own way.[27]

Her research shows that successful women were not conforming to the male stereotype but were daring to take their own path, a new path that often produced better results than the traditional path. We do not have to lead the way men lead. We can be creative and can do things in a manner that suits us and is more aligned with our values.

---

27 Julia Boorstin, "The Most Successful Women CEOs Lead Differently. Here's What We Can Learn from Them." LinkedIn, October 13, 2022, https://www.linkedin.com/pulse/most-successful-women-ceos-lead-differently-heres-what-julia-boorstin/.

Boorstin has collated beautiful, inspiring stories showing female resilience. When these women are rejected from the establishment, they come back with full rigor to reform the same industries that shunned them. We have the example of Whitney Wolfe Herd, the founder of Bumble, who, at twenty-five, was pushed out of Tinder but was quick to jump back up again to create a platform that empowered women to make the first move.

These women were not shying away from bringing more empathy and compassion into their workplaces and creating a more human-centric culture for innovation—women like Toyin Ajayi, who is reinventing the healthcare system through Cityblock Health, innovating sustainable solutions instead of short-term fixes.

Equally refreshing is seeing these women elevate purpose to the same level as profit and demonstrate that it is possible to make decisions that have a positive impact on the environment and the societies where we live. And precisely because of the focus on purpose, these companies perform better as they attract more customers and talent.[28]

Broostin's work is groundbreaking and came at a time when I really needed to see that women can in fact thrive through their unique characteristics, not despite them. These are women

---

28   Julia Boorstin, "The Most Successful Women CEOs Lead Differently. Here's What We Can Learn from Them." LinkedIn, October 13, 2022, *https://www.linkedin.com/pulse/most-successful-women-ceos-lead-differently-heres-what-julia-boorstin/*.

leaders who stuck to their guns, did things their own way, and delivered exceptional results, despite the headwinds.

This research strengthens my belief that women need to embrace creativity to push boundaries and create new groundbreaking solutions. One of the biggest drawbacks of conformity culture is that it represses creativity and innovation. When employees are rewarded for conformity and penalized for going against norms, we are discouraging risk-taking. When we don't take risks, we do not innovate, and that is often the beginning of demise for many businesses.

There is diversity among all of us. Let's normalize being ourselves at work, which means being able to laugh loudly, or wear bold lipstick, or get teary-eyed at everything because it is that time of the month. The less we as a group conform, the more normal we make it to be a woman at work.

A Valuable Lesson on Inclusion: Believe Other People's Experiences

After the experience with Val when he repeatedly asked me to leave a meeting and do other work for him, I came home and expressed my irritation to my husband. My husband, with his very logical mind, began to explore reasons for why Val had been doing what he was doing, coming up with excuses for his behavior, trying to make me feel that perhaps it was not personal.

I felt more and more frustrated. I simply wanted someone to understand how it felt to be excluded and dismissed in this way, especially as someone who knew she was different (being a woman in a male-dominated environment and also ethnically different). I simply wanted my experience validated.

When someone shares an experience at work where they feel excluded or unfairly treated, the logical brain response is to dismiss it: "Oh, you are reading too much into it. It was probably nothing," or "They probably did not mean it that way," or "They were having a bad day."

Perhaps this is because we would like to believe that there was no ill intention. Or we may think it may help our friend feel better if they knew that what happened was not personal, that there might be other factors at play. Regardless, when my husband started defending Val, I felt he was rejecting my reality. As a result of his attempt to help me see the other side or be "rational," not be too "dramatic" or "emotional" (labels women often receive), what I ended up hearing is "I don't believe you. Your experience, your feelings are not valid. Let's replace them with another reality, a reality we can live with, a reality that's more comfortable."

As painful as it was to be dismissed at work in this way by Val, it was an important lesson on empathy and compassion for marginalized employees at work. As a leader, I want to make sure that no one I work with ever feels like I did. In this experience, I found my purpose, creating an inclusive workplace where everyone has a voice and space to contribute.

Due to fear of being perceived to be a victim, I did not call Val out or talk to my boss, or HR, or anyone who could help me. I was too afraid that people would see me as weak. I did not want to be someone who could be victimized in that way. I did not want to give in to the stereotype of women being emotional and overly dramatic. So I kept quiet and made sure to not cross paths with Val again.

In retrospect, taking ownership would have meant daring to have uncomfortable conversations with Val and those around me instead of brushing it under the rug. If I had shown up as a leader, I would have taken the risk of being seen as overly dramatic. A leader sets boundaries on how they are treated. A leader holds other people accountable. I did not muster the courage to do that in this instance, but it is a lesson I take with me into all my new roles.

We learn from each experience. The experience with Val was the first of its kind for me, and it taught me that only I can advocate for myself. I cannot expect that others will notice, and I cannot expect others to know how I am feeling. When I do not bring such microaggressions to the surface, when I do not openly talk about how they make me feel, I am denying myself the opportunity to find allies. It does not have to be an act of rebellion; it can be an act of love for myself and for others around me and an opportunity to build connection.

Instead of framing negative experiences as "I am a victim in the situation," which then prevents me from speaking up,

I can reframe them as "I am a leader (and therefore not a victim), and I am speaking up to change the culture, to ensure that others do not experience the same exclusion behavior. I am the driver of change."

Diversity, equity, and inclusion is not a side issue that we can solve with one-off trainings. It is a core aspect of leadership and high-performance culture and is one of the leading predictors of attrition at the workplace. When employees do not feel that they can bring their whole selves to work or are penalized for challenging the status quo, if given a choice, they will find a workplace that's more accepting of them. It is simply not enough to hire diverse candidates; we need to systematically work on our work culture to reduce the pressures to conform and be comfortable with dissenting points of view and the friction they may create so we can reap the benefits of a diverse workforce. Lastly, we need to speak up when we are faced with microaggressions, and we need to find allies or be those allies for others in the workplace. Believe people's experiences so that you can work toward creating a more inclusive workplace.

Chapter 10:
Setting Boundaries

You get what you tolerate.

— *Henry Cloud*

Boundaries are agreements and explicit communication of what is desired, what is acceptable, and what is not acceptable. In an authoritative leadership style, boundaries are not always apparent, and the consequences of crossing a boundary can be grave. However, as an agile leader, communicating boundaries is essential. Effective autonomous teams operate in the parameters of clear boundaries that channel them into a specific direction and guide them forward. These boundaries are often set collaboratively. They are clearly communicated and are not used to assert power and control over others.

As a leader, you set your boundaries and allow your team to set boundaries with you. Tell them what is okay and what is not okay; for example, "It is okay to call me for urgent matters after work, but everything else can be sent through email or text." Boundaries are great to establish early on in a team so there are agreements on how to behave with each other. Team boundaries can be set collaboratively, where the team decides together how they would like to be treated and operate. You can create a set of values or rules and hang them on the wall. Make sure to review them often so that everyone is reminded of what they have agreed on.

Being Assertive

Mia is an executive leader at one of the leading technology companies in Europe. A year ago, we were sitting together in a leadership retreat exploring our strengths. In one of our reflective exercises, she was struggling to articulate her strength. The rest of us could see it clearly in everything she did, but she was having trouble identifying it on her own. We all mirrored back to her what we saw, and she was astonished.

Mia had an incredible talent for planning for the long term, assessing different scenarios, and being there to ensure that everyone and everything would be okay. We told her, "You embody this immense love for the planet, and you have the incredible ability to think strategically, plan, and see what systems need to be in place so that our goals are met."

Her response was, "Doesn't everyone think like this?"

Knowing her strength was transformational for her. She reflected deeply on the insights and allowed herself to sink into who she was and not hold back. She began to envision what more she could do with her natural talents. She was interviewing for new roles, and she noticed an immediate shift in her confidence and ability to express what she wanted.

She was no longer responding to the interview questions based on her best guesses of what the company or interviewer wanted to hear. Instead, she was responding from a place of what she believed and what was right for her. She was no longer trying to sell herself to get roles; instead, she was being completely herself and expressing what she was good at and what she wanted. Only after she understood what she wanted and who she was did it become clear to her what role she would accept. The power dynamics shifted. For the first time, she felt like she was in the driver's seat, deciding what role was right for her.

When Mia began to clearly express what she wanted, the world shifted to make room, and she took a quantum leap in her career. She was presented with more possibilities, and eventually she said yes to an exciting new role as CEO of a company whose purpose was deeply connected with hers.

In her story, I saw the power of believing in oneself and being assertive. Mia used that rock-solid inner belief in herself to communicate what she wanted with confidence. Being assertive means that you take away the filters and express your needs and feelings clearly and firmly, without disrespecting others. You are not rude; you are clear. When you are assertive, you are not undermining yourself or others.

You are not second-guessing your needs based on how you will be perceived. Being assertive is particularly important in job interviews, where we state our needs, what we would like a job to do for us. It is also important in our relationship with our bosses and those who report to us, where we come up with clear agreements on roles and responsibilities.

Here are my top tips on how you can start showing up more assertively today.

1. Before going into important discussions, prepare by listing the things that are most important to you. For example, if you are going to a job interview, jot down what your nonnegotiables are:
   o What is important to you in your new manager?
   o What is important to you with regard to the role and responsibilities?
   o What culture drives you to your highest performance?
   o What are your true strengths and weaknesses that you want your employer to accept you for?
   o Where would you like to grow?
2. Once you have clarity on what exactly it is that you want, make sure to express that in your discussion in as clear a way as possible. Don't be ambiguous; make sure your needs are understood.
3. Practice things that can be difficult for you to say beforehand. For example, for me, it is always hard to talk about money or to clearly state my rate or desired

salary. I practice saying these things a few times before calls or meetings so they begin to roll off my tongue more easily.

4. Don't overexplain. Don't use filler words or try to dilute your message.

5. Maintain eye contact. Sit up straight with your shoulders back to display confidence.

6. Listen carefully to the other person and, if needed, reiterate what is important to you.

Set Boundaries with Your Team as an Agile Leader

Boundaries are protections that are necessary for us to continue with our mission with love and compassion for others and ourselves.

As a parent, I learned that my children need boundaries to feel safe. I am continuously balancing the freedom I give them so that they can make mistakes and learn with setting firm boundaries that make them safe. I have learned that having rules and routines around mealtimes, bedtimes, homework time, and screen time creates predictability, reduces anxiety, and, in general, is healthier for the children. My child will express his anger and disagree, but I know that, while their self-expression is important, so is their sense of security. When the parent gives in, the child loses track of the boundaries. They feel a false sense of power over the adult at the cost of their sense of security. They find themselves without guardrails. This loss of sense of security can manifest in their behavior in different ways.

Setting boundaries with your team and at work is not the same as setting boundaries with your children, but it is a similar concept of creating an environment where there is some level of predictability and psychological safety. Essential to agile leadership is creating room for the team to experiment, make mistakes, and learn. Setting boundaries allows the team to take risks while making clear what kind of behavior is not tolerated, such as disrespecting a team member or a client, continuously arriving late for meetings, or not being prepared for important meetings. While autonomy is synonymous with freedom, it is not pure anarchy. Your team will feel safer and more in control if you provide structure with regular touchpoints, rules, and processes so that employees know what to expect.

Ensure that the processes do not become overbearing and get in the way of the agile way of working. Even though I make an analogy here with children, at work you are dealing with adults. Every adult wants to be treated as an equal and would appreciate being part of setting rules and processes. This is particularly true if you are a young manager dealing with more experienced employees. They may not respond well to a very directive, authoritative style, and they may prefer to mutually agree on rules and boundaries.

Remember, boundaries will be challenged, and you have to be ready to assert them consistently. Otherwise, the boundary ceases to exist.

Set Boundaries with Your Manager as an Agile Leader

Clear boundaries with your manager ensure that you are not setting false expectations that you need to live up to, and they prevent you from reaching a state of burnout. Most people struggle to set boundaries with managers, and that was no different for me. I feared the implications of setting boundaries. I worried that, if they came out wrong or if I came on too strong, I might jeopardize my performance evaluation and chances of getting the next big promotion.

My inability to set boundaries caught up with me when I finally got a much sought-after VP role.

I was willing to say all the right things to get the role, with the false hope that once I was there I could actually enact change and be myself. I did not effectively communicate how I wanted to lead, and I did not assert boundaries and create clear agreements on how we would operate despite our differences.

I operated with the pretense that, instead of being clear on what I wanted, I could give and take. I thought that I could do a bit of what my boss wanted, make him happy but still be able to focus on what was most important to me. I was not transparent; I was trying to please my boss and stick to my values. It was a recipe for disaster, as I found out that I was not able to do either.

I had organized a collaborative goal-setting session with the team where we were to work on OKRs (a popular goal-setting methodology: Objectives and Key Results). I had been using OKRs for years and found the methodology to be the best way for the team to take ownership of their goals and work on them collaboratively. I invited my boss to the session. We had a productive session and everyone felt satisfied. Afterward, though, my boss took the input and created a new plan of action, taking out some things we had agreed on and added new objectives we had not discussed. Without discussing it with me first, he went directly to my team with this plan.

That was the point where I should have asserted a boundary. Yes, he was my boss, but this was my team. Since I did not assert a boundary the first time this happened, I gave him the signal that it was okay with me if he bypassed me. So he continued to operate in this manner, undermining my role.

I was not setting boundaries for how my boss should interact with my team for fear of stepping on his toes.

Everything crumbled. I was unhappy and disempowered, and my boss felt like I was not delivering according to his expectations. You might already realize that this is the story I shared in Chapter 1. I ended up being assigned a new role, and my boss took over my team.

Months later, a mentor asked me, "Nada, what did you learn? How would you face a similar situation again? Would you be more compromising?"

I reflected on this question for quite some time. My response was a resounding no; I wish I was more uncompromising. I had compromised on my boundaries. I learned my lesson the hard way and, since then, every time I take on a job or assignment, I set very clear agreements up front on my role and responsibilities. I am very clear on what I expect from the role; I am clear on how I will lead and operate; I am clear on what they can expect from me so that there is no room for misunderstanding or disappointment about mismatched expectations. It is better to overcommunicate then undercommunicate. Communication ensures that we are not setting false expectations that we need to live up to.

My New Approach for Setting Boundaries

I outline my new approach below:

1. Be Crystal Clear on Your Leadership Style and How You Perceive Your Role and Responsibilities

Lay out, from day one, how you plan to lead. Be clear on your leadership style, what it means to you, and how you plan on leading. Create space to discuss how you might have a different leadership style than your manager. We should be able to tolerate diversity of leadership.

Fear kept me from being clear with my manager in the past. Now I am more assertive. I know that I have real value to add with my leadership style, and it is important to me that I express it with confidence.

I overcommunicate around the roles and responsibilities of jobs I take on. This gives both parties an opportunity to make a better decision about whether we are a good fit. Recently, I considered an associate position at a small investment firm. I loved the idea of working with them to expand my horizons and learn about a new field. However, I was aware that the job required me to keep my head in spreadsheets, double-check the data, and ensure that there were no mistakes. While I love learning about the financial side of businesses and analyzing data, there are many other people who are better suited for that role. I expressed to the managing director that I was interested in becoming involved in external activities of building connections, scouting for deals, and coaching the teams in the portfolio. He realized that that was not what he needed at the time; his priority was to get someone who could work on the back office financial spreadsheets. I really wanted to find a way for us to work together and was extremely disappointed that our needs did not align, but I am past the phase in my life where I say whatever the hiring manager wants me to say so that I can get a job. Now I am more transparent about my strengths and weakness in order to make sure that a job is the right fit for me.

2. Set Clear Boundaries Early on and Collaboratively

Take the time to set boundaries together as a team and together with your manager. Here are some questions you may wish to consider to set boundaries:

- Where do each of you have autonomy, and where do you need to consult each other? Establishing this ensures that you are not stepping on each other's toes but are making space for collaboration.
- How will you update each other? To avoid micromanagement tendencies, make space to provide updates on the project on a regular basis and be clear about areas where you would like help or input.
- What will your system be for prioritization? Do not say yes to everything. Push back on work that is out of scope and that you do not have the capacity for.
- What is your availability? Clarify when is it okay to reach out to you after work. You can also tell your team to not hold any important meetings past 5 p.m., as you will not be available.
- How will you be treated? If you feel like you were treated unfairly or disrespectfully, you have to confront the issue. Otherwise, you are saying that it is okay for you to be treated that way.
- What should others expect from you in terms of responsiveness? Make it clear that you do not respond to emails right away, and that if something is urgent, they can call or send you a text.

Remember to reinforce the boundaries. When one of your boundaries is infringed, it is important to remind people of the boundary in a polite manner.

Do not let your inability to be assertive or to set boundaries cost you your job.

I was never really taught the concept of boundaries. As a woman, I have been conditioned to be nice and kind. Setting boundaries and being assertive is hard. I associate those things with being rigid, inflexible, and selfish. This feeling goes back to when I have been assertive in the past and people did not react well. I am afraid to offend others, and I suffer from people-pleasing syndrome, which has cost me my happiness.

I grew up in a culture where we are not assertive. Most Asian cultures are "high context," where you do not clearly state things for the sake of being polite, but rather you expect people to read between the lines and understand the context. I realize that I have been conditioned to communicate in indirect ways, which are more nuanced. I expect people to pick up my meaning from the context and coded messages that I am sending. I am married to a Norwegian, and it took me a few years to realize that sometimes you just have to state the obvious; you have to put it in words. People cannot read your mind, and those coded messages that I send my husband don't work so well!

Chapter 11:

Money Mindset

The security of playing it safe is not worth the pain of never knowing what it feels like to be truly alive.

— *Cory Muscara*

Growing up in Pakistan, I saw people in school who had far more money than we did, and I saw children on the street who had to beg for a living. It is the dichotomy of growing up in the developing world, wanting more yet being grateful for what we have.

One of my most vivid memories is of going to the store with my mom and staring at the shiny golden wrapping of a chewy caramel chocolate bar called Jubilee behind the glass display. I wanted it so badly, yet I was engulfed in fear. Should I ask for it and face that stern no? I knew we could not afford it, but the temptation was so strong.

I actually don't remember if I asked for it or if I got it. I just remember the longing and the frustration of not being able to ask for what I wanted.

If you grew up in scarcity, you can probably relate. Like Pavlov's dog, we were conditioned. We learned not to ask for what we want—especially not money, not more money. Scarcity mindset is a belief that wealth, resources, and opportunities are limited and never enough. This mindset is perpetuated by the unhealthy (often very masculine) competitive environments in which we operate, built on the presumption that there is simply not enough to go around. We make ourselves believe that if our colleague gets a raise or a promotion, they are taking from a limited pot and there are less opportunities for us. Abundance mindset, on the other hand, is the belief that resources are unlimited. It allows us to view the world from an optimistic framing. If my colleague can get a promotion, so can I. Possibilities are endless. What if we were to adopt an abundance mindset not only for opportunities, but also for money? What if we were to believe that there is enough for everyone, that we can start asking and striving for more?

My friend's colleague recently started a new job, and she could not contain her excitement when we met up for coffee. She spoke about all the fun things she would do and how amazing this new opportunity was. I echoed her enthusiasm and added, "And I bet you are getting a huge raise too!"

At that, though, she mellowed down her excitement and said with a straight face, "That is not important to me. That is not the reason why I changed jobs." She was willing to celebrate the new job, but not the raise. It is like an unspoken rule: women do not talk about money, and God forbid that anyone thinks we are motivated by money!

Women and Money

Most of us will cruise through our careers and make decent money and be happy. And that is just fine. But if your ambition is to create more impact in the world, more money means more power, influence, and freedom in your life. Money allows you to have a better quality of life as you pursue a demanding career. It allows you to afford luxuries like childcare and cleaning help at home, so you can focus on tasks where you are indispensable.

Mara Harvey, a renowned economist and author, appeared on my podcast, *Braving Innovation*, to share her work on pushing for more financial literacy amongst young girls and women. She points out that women make active decision in household finances when it comes to groceries and paying the babysitter and the cleaner. But when it comes to bigger decisions related to mortgages and investments, we leave a lot of those decisions to our partners. Women who are single or divorced usually find themselves unequipped to deal with financial decisions because they were not involved in these decisions earlier.[29]

---

29   Nada Ahmed, interview with Mara Harvey, "E17: Dr. Mara Harvey on Financial Literacy, Taking Control of Our Finances and What We Can Teach Our Kids," September 11, 2022, in Braving Innovation, podcast, MP3 audio, 37:37, *https://nadahmed.podbean.com/e/e16-dr-mara-harvey-on-financial-literacy-taking-control-of-our-finances-and-what-we-can-teach-our-kids/*.

Many women express indifference or have deep-rooted insecurities when it comes to dealing with money and financial decisions. We need to actively work to counter this attitude within ourselves so we can built a new future that is more equitable. Let's get curious and learn how money works.

Last year, I started a mastermind group with powerful women who invest in venture capital. (You can find more information about the mastermind group here: https://www.nadahmed. com/mastermind) Finally, I found women who unabashedly spoke about their desire to make more money. We don't aspire to make money so that we can buy a Ferrari or a fancy bag; we want to make money so we have more freedom in life to use our time the way we want, so we can work on those influential projects that will advance the causes we feel strongly about. Money is freedom. Money is power.

While I was successful at corporate and felt deeply passionate about my work, I also felt that my job was limiting me in many ways. What if I was to quit and have a go at something bigger? My mind opened up to taking bigger risks and making more money. It requires courage to let go of the stability of the salary trickling in every month. A job pays you just enough to keep you in the rat race, and it make you dependent on the salary like a drug. The progression is slow, and it is rarely ever enough to make you independent of your job. A job is a safe path that gives you a false sense of security—false because you can lose your job at any moment.

I am on a journey of disrupting my own money mindset, and I decided to get out of the rat race that was not getting me much further financially. I figured, how about risking the stability of the monthly salary to have a go at my dream life?

Salary Negotiation

The conventional belief is that women negotiate less than men, and while that may have been true historically, new data suggests that this is changing. Women are now negotiating as much as men, yet they are not getting the desired outcomes. In one study, it was found that a greater percentage of women than men (64 percent to 59 percent) asked for raises and promotions, but women were turned down twice as often as men.[30] These numbers suggest deep unconscious bias in the system against women asking for more. Asking for more money requires us to be assertive, and, as discussed in the last chapter, assertiveness is not a desired quality in a woman at work. When women exhibit stereotypically masculine traits commonly associated with leadership, such as assertiveness, they are less liked when compared with men exhibiting the same traits.[31] There is plenty of work for us to do to dismantle

---

30   *Laura Kray and Margaret Lee, "The Pay Gap for Women Starts with a Responsibility Gap," Wall Street Journal, October 14, 2021, https://www. wsj.com/articles/the-pay-gap-for-women-starts-with-a-responsibility-gap-11634224762.*

31   "The Double-Bind Dilemma for Women in Leadership: Damned If You Do, Doomed If You Don't (Report)," Catalyst, July 15, 2007, *https://www.catalyst. org/research/the-double-bind-dilemma-for-women-in-leadership-damned-if-you-do-doomed-if-you-dont/.*

these biases on the societal and organization levels. We can start by continuing to raise this issue, checking our own biases, and continuing to negotiate assertively and tactfully.

When I got my first job after my master's, I was so ecstatic to finally get a job offer that negotiating the salary was the last thing on my mind. My sister, who was in business school at that time, gave me a serious pep talk. She said, "Negotiate every single time! You may not get what you want, but one, you will get better at negotiation, and two, you will always learn something. Use it as an opportunity to get more information that you can then use in your next round of negotiations."

I have never forgotten her wise words, and I have made it a point to negotiate every single time, even if doing so is uncomfortable. I have not always gotten the results I wanted, but every negotiation gets me much-needed practice.

I had assumed that managers don't like people asking for raises and want to avoid such conversations until I became a boss and realized how wrong I was. I respected my team for speaking up about their desires to be paid more. I found raise requests to be completely normal conversations, and I was grateful that my team members let me know if they were feeling undervalued. I also understood the courage that it takes to ask for a raise. I know I myself spent hours prepping for such talks. I did not perceive my team members as greedy, ungrateful, or too proud (I feared being perceived in that way) when they asked for raises; in fact, I respected them more for it. Being on the other side made me realize that I did not need to be scared or uncomfortable negotiating for myself. When I do, I am simply being open and honest and giving my manager the opportunity to make fair salary adjustments.

Once, I was hiring an exceptional leader for my team, and I knew that we would have to pay him more than I made as his manager. That did not bother me at that time. I was committed to the team objectives, and I wanted to hire the best talent. As time went by and my salary did not budge despite me bringing it up several times, though, I became resentful. I felt that my boss was not willing to fight for me the way I was willing to fight for my team. If you settle for less than what you deserve and see others getting paid more, it will eventually get to you. Ask for your fair share from the beginning to avoid resentment later.

If your employer really cannot budge, have them make a plan or give you a timeline. Use questions like "What is a path for me to get to a 20 percent raise?" That opens up your boss for a dialogue, and they may be more open to exploring different paths for you.

Let's stop leaving money on the table. Let's reframe: We are not being greedy when we *do* advocate for ourselves; we are simply asking for a fair share. We are not blindly chasing higher salaries; we are simply beginning to value money and the power that comes with it.

Financial Literacy

Most of us are not taught how to manage our finances, either in school or at home. In the book *Rich Dad, Poor Dad*, Robert T. Kiyosaki talks about how he grew up watching two dads have a very different relationship and mindset around money: his own dad, a working class dad, and his friend's dad, who was a rich dad. The difference comes down to working for money versus letting the money do the work for you.

Money was never my main motivation. I was driven by meaningful, impactful work, but I was also excited by prestige and titles (until I got the title I was chasing and realized that it did not mean as much to me as I thought it would). A title does not automatically give you influence, and you can get influence in other ways. Having lots of money, however, is quite influential if you use that money properly. Money is freedom. Money allows you to have the lifestyle you desire. It allows you to invest in companies you believe in, and it allows you to retire early from a job so you can start your own business.

I have learned a lot from my husband over the years, as he cares less about prestige and building a brand and has instead systematically and gradually accumulated more wealth than I have. He read *Rich Dad, Poor Dad* a few years ago and started implementing the learnings in his life. He also joined the FIRE (Financial Independence, Retire Early) movement.

FIRE is a movement focused on saving and investing enough money to retire early. The goal is to have an investment portfolio that can sustain you for the rest of your life, thereby allowing you to retire when you choose. To become financially independent, people usually refer to the 4 percent rule. The rule states that, from an investment portfolio, you should be able to withdraw 4 percent of the value every year, and it should last the rest of your lifetime. Four percent also equates to twenty-five times yearly expenses.

I know that not everyone is able to think so far ahead to retirement, but the point here is that you can move up retirement, particularly if you are not passionate about your job. You can stop working for money but work to make an impact and bring more joy to your life. The FIRE mindset allows you to think about how you can accumulate more wealth now, whether that is from making the right investments or figuring out additional sources of income.

To start on your road to financial independence or just better personal financial health, here are some quick tips:

1. Ask for more. Don't leave your share on the table. Negotiate your salary every opportunity you get.
2. Start investing, whether in the stock market or elsewhere. Make the money start working for you today. Simply carve out part of your monthly income to invest.

o You can start by investing in industries that you are most interested in or knowledgeable about (or would like to get more knowledgeable about). Use this as an opportunity to learn and invest.

3. Get curious about how finance works. If your partner currently manages the big financial decisions in your family, sit down with him or her and talk about where the money is going and how it is being invested. Explore together how you can make the money work for you.

4. Explore additional sources of income other than just your day job. Do your research and talk about options with friends and others who are more knowledgeable than you in this area. Get curious about making more money.

5. Celebrate the investments you're making. Share with your friends, and get comfortable talking about money.

Chapter 12:

Collaboration

Running a business is a team sport.

— Nada Ahmed

I was proud to have recruited a stellar team. I was particularly excited about Kim, who I had seen manage complex projects with great agility and ease at the consulting firm where he had worked before.

Over time, I found out that Kim was an amazing individual contributor and would stay up late producing amazing PowerPoint slides. He took his time, and they were a masterpiece when delivered. I assigned him the role of lead on our team strategy project, meaning that he would be creating a document that illustrated our collective thoughts on the way forward. I noticed that the team began to refer to the project as Kim's project and his strategy work, when in fact it was a team project. The team was not taking ownership. I pulled Kim aside and mentioned my concern to him. This project was not about creating the perfect strategy, but rather, a strategy that the team could take ownership for and feel accountable for during execution.

Kim pushed back and challenged me on the value of collaboration and stated that, at times, we overvalue collaboration. It slows us down. We cannot collaborate on everything. He claimed it would be more efficient if he put in extra hours and got the work done quicker.

Sure. Speed at the expense of collaboration.

It is easy to focus on speed because it creates an illusion of progress. It is quantifiable. *I am producing, I am executing.* We confuse speed with value-adding work and progress. We do not take the time to ensure that tasks are completed as a team. When the team truly collaborates, it takes ownership. When things go wrong, they do not point fingers at different departments for providing faulty specifications. Everyone in the team is a value-adding contributor who feels accountable for the deliverable. Leadership is being able to assume responsibility and not defer it. Blaming others for not achieving the objectives is an artifact of individualistic work culture.

After a few weeks, Kim came back to me and thanked me for challenging him. He realized that he had been shaped by the action-biased culture, where action mattered more than the outcome. He got creative about how to encourage more collaboration within the team. They began to take ownership and produced a strategy that the entire team could stand behind. It truly became the team's strategy that they felt proud of. I saw the team take responsibility for its actual implementation and gain significant influence in the organization as they executed flawlessly. Everyone noticed not just the team but Kim's ability to show up as a collaborative leader. Within a year, he was offered a promotion to lead an important strategic team in the company.

Over and over, I see the benefits of working together as a group to produce something, even if it's less perfect than perhaps it could be, versus creating a masterpiece that only one person has ownership to. Collaboration is not easy. It is hard to measure and hard to fabricate, but it is always worth the effort. It may seem to slow us down in the short term, but it accelerates progress over the long term. It allows us to go further.

One of the most effective collaborations I experienced was when I took part in Seth Godin's altMBA.

The altMBA workshop gave me many lessons on collaboration. It is a four-week program, and each week, you have a different team of four to five people to work with. The assignments were challenging for the time available, and we were reminded that the goal was not only to get each assignment finished, but to finish it in a collaborative manner.

During one assignment, I did not notice that some on the team were not participating. After some time, one of our nonparticipants spoke up and expressed that she found our process a bit overwhelming. She was not able to keep up with what was being said. She did not want to be a bystander, and she suggested that we try a new approach where everyone could be part of the process. We were grateful that she spoke up and stopped us from continuing in a way that prioritized speed over collaboration. Together, we came up with a different approach that made it easier for everyone to contribute. She reflected later on how effectively collaborating impacted her and the outcome:

> The atmosphere became much more playful and creative. It was wonderful to build upon each other's ideas, to be inspired by something another person said, and to get into a flow of coming up with new suggestions. We had a lot of laughter along the way, which felt good and built connection with the team. Ideas emerged that we'd never have thought of if doing this alone and without others to bounce thoughts off.

> We learnt to take more time at the start of the session to arrive, to check in with each other, to decide how we would work and what we wanted to achieve. It is easy to let the time constraint get in the way. To feel there wasn't time for discussion, we just needed to get on with it.

Collaboration is a conscious decision, and we cannot rely on hope that it will be initiated organically, especially when we are conditioned to optimize individual performance.

Speed matters because it creates momentum, and I use it tactfully in my design thinking process that I have developed to get teams to innovate and test ideas faster. Yet I ensure that collaboration is intrinsic in that process. The price of not collaborating during the strategy and goal-setting phase is usually paid during execution. It will show up in misunderstandings of the objectives, lack of buy-in and commitment, and team failure to take ownership for the project. Sound familiar?

Collaborative work environments are inclusive, they are more fun for everyone involved, and they create high-performance teams instead of high-performance individuals.

Agile Leadership Guiding Principles on How to Collaborate Better

In most work cultures, we reward individual wins over team goals and results over teamwork and relationships. We get so hung up on trying to meet predefined KPIs that we lose sight of the direction or even whether we are making any progress at all. Meeting our goals should be as much about the journey, about *how* we meet those goals—it should not just be about meeting the numbers, but meeting the numbers in a way that leads to long-term sustainability of the business.

Here are some of the guiding principles I use to collaborate better in teams.

- Set the tone early on for how you will work and make it clear that collaboration is a priority. This takes time in the beginning, but it is more effective in the long term.

- Be creative around KPIs that encourage collaboration and teamwork. For example, set shared goals and evaluate individual performance based on how collaboratively goals were achieved.
- Recognize when you are personally feeling competitive toward others on your team and make a genuine effort to collaborate with those people by offering your help in achieving their goals.

Early in my career, I was very competitive. I sized myself up against everyone. I felt threatened by others. I was driven by a scarcity mindset that made me believe that there was only room for one leader. As I got more experienced, I noticed the benefits of collaborative thinking and working toward shared goals collaboratively, when there was not one dominant player but rather the whole team played equal roles. It made me feel safe, not threatened. No one is a threat in the workplace until you start seeing them as such. I acknowledge my competitive side—many of us have one. But today, as soon as I feel threatened, I take a deep breath and repeat to myself that collaboration is the key to success. Then I take action with a genuine attempt to collaborate. I offer to help someone with their goal; I offer my friendship to the person I am feeling threatened by; I ask to go out to lunch with the person I am seeing as my competition. Soon, I feel the competitive spirit dissipate, and we find ways to mutually benefit one another.

When you choose collaboration first, you will find yourself in a positive and uplifting energy at work that is inspiring, less threatening, and more empowering. Try it!

Chapter 13:

Feedback Culture

If you are not in the arena getting your ass kicked on occasion, I am not interested in or open to your feedback.

— *Brené Brown*

Feedback is critical to agile leadership. It helps us to continuously improve the process, the product, the team performance, and our leadership.

When I took on a big leadership role, the book *Radical Candor* by Kim Scott was my bible. I was constantly referring to it for guidance on how to give feedback and create a culture where feedback can help improve performance. My key takeaway from the book was that feedback is not about what people are doing wrong, it is about how I can help them become even better versions of themselves.

As a leader, it was important to me to look out for what my team was doing well. Most people do not even know what they are good at. I learned to be specific with positive feedback. Instead of a simple "Amazing presentation today!", I would say something like, "I loved your presentation today. You started with a story that got all of us immediately into the context of the problem you are solving, and you ended with very clear conclusions and recommendations. You gave us so much clarity that we were able to make decisions quickly and take action."

We admire our colleagues in our heads, but we often do not express that admiration to them. Make it a habit to tell your team what you appreciate about them, and be specific about what they did and the impact they had.

As a leader, I want my team to know that I appreciate them for their strengths and for who they are. I do not want them to feel that I am constantly looking for things they are doing wrong. Building a culture of positive feedback builds trust and makes it easier to give feedback on what is not working and needs improvement.

Pitfall of Feedback Culture

A feedback culture is one in which we regularly solicit, give, and receive feedback so we are continuously improving, learning, and growing. However, most managers do not know how to give effective feedback, and if given the wrong way, feedback can do more harm than good.

Obnoxious feedback, for example, creates a toxic culture that thwarts innovation and adversely impacts your diversity and inclusion goals. If you want to advocate for a healthy feedback culture, you need proper training on how to give and receive feedback. Most of us really struggle to dissociate our self-worth from the judgment that is being passed on to us in the form of feedback because feedback is just that—a judgment, one person's perspective of another. It is important that we frame feedback properly, check our own biases, and invite input from the person we are giving feedback to.

Feedback is not about changing a person to be more like us. The goal is to help them grow and find their own way that is authentic to them. As leaders, we are not trying to change people; we are making them better versions of themselves. If people feel forced to change, they will feel stuck and unhappy. Instead, frame the feedback session as a discussion on how you can find a path forward that makes both parties happy.

Receiving Feedback

In our modern work environment, where we put feedback on a pedestal, many managers feel entitled to give critical feedback constantly. Always ask yourself, "What is their intention?" If their true intention is not to help you, thank them and move on. Learn to take feedback from everyone but not let it take an ounce of your energy and enthusiasm away from your goals and dreams.

Early on in my career, I was constantly seeking feedback. It was a function of my insecurity, looking for that validation, that confirmation, that I was doing okay. Not only was I looking for approval or praise, I was also asking the wrong people for feedback. I have learned to be more judicious about who I seek feedback from. I value feedback from people I respect and who respect me back and will have something valuable to contribute. These are people who I look up to, who I aspire to be like, and who are my role models. I put less value on feedback from people who hardly know me, who do not connect with my dreams and aspirations, and who will not be cheering for me on my journey. For example, if I were looking for feedback on a new podcast, I would not ask my boss who never listens to podcasts, has no interest in them, and would herself never want to create one. I would instead ask my friend who I trust and who has a successful podcast and can give advice based on her experience.

Tips on How to Receive Critical Feedback

1. When receiving critical feedback at work, distance yourself as much as possible during the conversation. I like to imagine that the feedback is about a third person. This allows me to get detached and keep my emotions at bay.

2. Get curious. Don't just have the other person stop at their first sentence. Do not assume that you know what they mean—ask questions. Say, "Can you explain that?" "Tell me more," "I am not sure I understand,'" or "Can you give me an example?" The more you get the feedback-giver to talk, the better. Focusing on asking questions keeps you from getting defensive and really giving the word to the giver as you try to digest what they are saying.

3. Once they are done giving you feedback, remember that you do not have to respond right away. It is okay to say, "I need some time to process this feedback; can we circle back on this tomorrow?" This is often a good strategy, as it gives you time to really assess how you want to respond to the feedback.

4. Once you have time to process the feedback, circle back. Try not to be defensive, but if you have a different point of view, express it with confidence. There are many ways of looking at a problem or issue. The feedback-giver may not have all the facts and may have been looking at the issue from a place of bias or a judgmental viewpoint. It's okay to be grateful for the feedback and still counter it with your own perspective.

5. If you see that there are ways for you to improve based on the feedback, state them and discuss them (especially if the person giving feedback is your manager).

6. Make sure to thank the feedback-giver, especially if you feel that they gave you feedback respectfully and had the best intentions in mind.

7. After the feedback conversation, you have a choice. You can decide to disregard the feedback if you do not think it helps you achieve your goal or become the leader you want to be, or you can identify steps you can take to improve.

Most importantly, do not let any critical feedback impact your self-esteem and confidence. I know that this is easier said than done, but if you aspire to lead, you will have to put yourself out there. This makes you susceptible to criticism and feedback; there is no avoiding it. Take the feedback for what's it worth, learn from it, and move on.

Giving Feedback

My friend Sukaina told me a story about a time when she worked on a very difficult assignment with a tight deadline. "I worked day and night to get it to my boss by the end of the day on Friday. I was exhausted by the time I handed it in." She realized that she did not have enough time to analyze all the data in detail, but she did what she could to have the presentation ready in time.

Her boss took one look at it and said, "This is not good enough." and walked off.

Sukaina held back tears. That was the last thing she needed to hear. She knew that the presentation wasn't perfect, and she knew it could be better, but she had put her heart and soul into getting it to him on time.

How effective was the boss's feedback? Was a soul-crushing response helping Sukaina to be better or ensuring a better outcome the next time? Sukaina knew exactly what she could do better if she had more time. Her boss did not have to tell her or point it out. His feedback was simply not helpful and lacked empathy. An agile leader would give Sukaina the space to explain where her work was weak. He would make the time to go over it properly and identify what she would do better next time if she had more time. He would give her a pat on the back, recognize her hard work, and tell her to go home and get some rest. To use feedback as a learning opportunity, there needs to be a foundation of trust, and on that Friday afternoon, the lack of empathy from Sukaina's boss blew away any speck of trust that had ever existed.

I recommend immediate feedback, but I also believe that timing is important. In Sukaina's case, harsh, immediate feedback was the last thing she needed. Her boss could have easily waited until Monday, when he had more time to discuss how the presentation could be better. I believe that, as leaders, we should operate with the assumption that everyone is doing their best. No one purposely wants to do bad work. If Sukaina's boss operated with that mindset, he would have waited until Monday to have a proper debrief instead of making a quick comment on Friday when she was exhausted and perhaps not in the best state to assess the weakness in her work.

Feedback as a manager is not about the giver, but about the receiver. I always ask myself, "How will the person benefit? How is this valuable to them?" I ask myself, "Is this something that I just want to get off my chest?" Feedback is not about telling people the first thing that comes to our minds. As leaders, our job is not to "fix" people so that they meet our preferences. Feedback is not about getting them to change their behavior simply because it bothers us. Feedback should not be coming from a place of irritation. When we are irritated, that is something inside of us that we need to address; it is not something that the person in front of us needs to fix.

Without proper guidance, we throw our judgments around, masquerading them as feedback. Unfortunately, this disproportionately impacts diverse employees. Employees who do not fit the stereotype and those who think and do things differently bear the brunt of this feedback culture. They are told over and over again to conform, to be like everyone else, because "that is normal around here." Feedback is not about picking at everything that makes a person unique; instead, it's about helping them achieve their goals for themselves in a way that benefits the business.

Here are some of my leadership tips on how to give feedback:

1. Get to know your team members individually. What are their dreams and ambitions, and what areas would they like to grow in? Feedback needs to be specific to each individual, and it should not be about you and your comfort but about how you can help them unleash their potential.
2. Feedback conversations need to be a dialogue where you are genuinely curious about the other person's perspective. Make space for a dialogue instead of passing down judgments.
3. Avoid judgments that are solely based on your perspective, who you are, and your own metrics for

success and performance. Ask yourself whether you are trying to make the other person more like you.

4. Keep feedback discussions separate from performance review and evaluation sessions. Connecting feedback to employees' performance and career development can be quite harmful for employee morale. When feedback is given in these contexts, it can feel like an ultimatum ("Do as I say or you will not get promoted."). Instead, feedback should be provided on a regular basis, whenever you notice something that needs improvement. Do not wait until the end of the quarter, when you have a meeting scheduled, to weigh in.

5. Don't give feedback on someone's personality. Make your feedback about the work, not the person.

6. Always ask if a person wants feedback or advice from you before giving it. You are not entitled to give anyone feedback. If the person responds no, that means that you have some trust-building work to do as a leader.

7. Be specific. Avoid being generic. Talk about a particular incident that happened instead of making general statements like "You are always late to meetings."

8. Focus on positive feedback. There is extensive research showing that negative feedback rarely leads to improvement and that positive reinforcement works better for overall performance.[32] Positive feedback

---

32 Paul Green, "Shopping for Confirmation: How Disconfirming Feedback Shapes Social Networks," Harvard Business School Working Paper No. 18-028, September 20, 2017, http://dx.doi.org/10.2139/ssrn.3040066.

increases perceived self-efficacy and confidence in people's ability to achieve their goals.

Too often, I see people of authority using feedback as an excuse to push people down. This comes from a place of ego, where we think we know better. An effective feedback session is a healthy dialogue where judgment is kept at bay. An agile leader avoids using power or authority to get people to improve or grow. Instead, they guide and coach their teams in a manner that activates the employees' intrinsic motivation to do better.

Chapter 14:

Brand Yourself

Brand yourself for the career you want, not the job you
have.

— Dan Schawbel

I took the Gallup StrengthsFinder test a few years ago and
discovered that one of my top five strengths was Significance.
People with this strength have a strong desire to make a
difference, to live a life that influences other people, and to
work on projects that will have a lasting impact on society. It is
important for me to live with a purpose and to work on projects
that will drive real change. So you can imagine my frustration
when I ended up at a job where I had almost nothing to do. I
felt useless and redundant. I wanted to be put on projects that
were strategic and creating significant impact. Instead, I felt
excluded from everything.

It took me a few weeks before I saw the wonderful opportunity
in the situation. Wait a second. I am getting paid a decent
salary, and no one really cares how I spend my time?!

Consider yourself lucky if you have such a job because today, you have more resources available than ever before to help you learn, build your own brand, and potentially start your own business.

When it dawned on me that this was an opportunity to really get creative in designing my own work, my own goals, and my own schedule, I got really excited.

I drafted two big goals: 1. Find a new job that was meaningful, and 2. Learn and grow.

I created a self-growth plan with a list of things I wanted to get better at. One was public speaking, and the other was gaining knowledge within innovation and technology. I used LinkedIn as a tool to advance my goals. I began by making short videos where I shared my thoughts and perspective on topics that interested me. I signed up for networking events, conferences, and seminars. I volunteered to speak on topics that I aspired to be an expert in. Within a matter of months, I was no longer an aspiring expert; I *was* an expert. People began to recognize me and I was able to build immediate connections based on the content I shared online.

But then something even more surprising happened. People began to view me as someone who was rocking her new role. They would say things like "It is great to watch your ascension. You have done so well for yourself. It seems like the new job really suits you well. It has really given you the opportunities you needed to reach your potential."

My initial reaction was that people were getting it all wrong. My job was not great, and this was *not* the best thing that had ever happened to me in my career. Quite the opposite . . .

But then I realized that this was the true power of social media. It can be used to completely misconstrue reality, or it can be used to create your own reality. I used that to my own advantage.

It did not matter how my job was going, where I was working, or what I was doing at work. Through social media, I could take the reins of my career, take charge of the narrative, and build my own personal brand. I was emboldened. I did not need my employer's stamp of approval. I could hold my own with my very own personal brand.

What Building a Brand Did for Me

At the start, I simply wanted to build my confidence and find my voice by posting on LinkedIn and speaking at events. Over time, I saw the impact of putting myself out there and the power of my emerging personal brand. I started being invited to exclusive events. I got introduced to other amazing people who were on the same journey as me. I was encouraged by the results I was seeing, so I continued posting and volunteering to speak at events. Eventually, people paid me for speaking gigs. I got asked to be on influential company boards (positions that are not normally open to the public), and ultimately, I got the job I wanted, which was my main goal. But it did not stop there. I got promoted within the company because of my brand, I made more money because of it, and my self-esteem skyrocketed.

I became a mentor at startup accelerators, created my own tech and digital leadership networks, started to organize events, and connected with prominent professionals in my space. I realized that you can learn and grow plenty outside your job!

By the end of that one year, even while I was working a job where I struggled to find a place for myself inside the company, I turned outwards and built a brand and a place for myself outside the company. Within a matter of months, I had not only gotten my ideal job as head of innovation at a leading engineering company, but I had presented at over fifteen conferences. My public speaking skills were improving, and I had built an incredible network.

Branding through Social Media

Social media is not the only way to build a brand, but today, it's the easiest and most effective way to reach more people and build a digital reputation. I used social media for what's it worth, as an empowering tool to build a personal brand and to create a community outside my workplace.

It may seem daunting to put your voice out there when you feel inexperienced and unsure about yourself. But all brands started from somewhere. Instead of focusing on being judged, think about what building a brand can do for you. Let it open doors and amplify your impact.

Early on in my career, I didn't think that I had anything to offer or anything to build my brand around. I was still finding my voice and discovering what I felt passionate about. But with social media, it is never too early or too late to get started. See it as an experiment. You get to choose your personal brand, so think about what life experiences you want to bring to your brand, how do you want to present yourself, and the skills you have acquired throughout your career. Brand is about what people should know you for, your area of expertise, and when they should reach out to you. Ask yourself, "What values do I stand for? Why would people want to associate with my brand?"

If you are working as a project manager or an analyst at a bank, start talking about your experiences on social media. What are you learning? Share with others. You want people to know what you stand for, what you care about, and what your competencies and knowledge areas are. It will not only help you get more customers, but it will also attract opportunities outside your current business or employer.

Choose the content type that you are most comfortable with. For example, if you like writing, write blogs and posts. If you find it easier to make videos or share memes, that is fine too. Try to stay consistent with your themes and to be authentic to who you are. Your goal is to earn the trust and respect of others in the industry. As long as you are sharing valuable content, people will follow and engage.

Branding through Building Your Network

If social media is not your thing, an alternative and complementary way to build your brand is through building a network. Personal brand is your reputation, and you are building it through the work that you do and the interactions you have. You can expand the reach of your reputation by being more visible, being present in the right arenas, connecting with people of influence, and having conversations that show your area of expertise. Here are some tips for building a brand through growing your network:

1. Find opportunities for speaking engagements or panel discussions where you can discuss important topics that matter to you and exhibit who you are, your expertise, and what you believe in.
2. Engage in projects outside your core team and outside your company. That way, people can get to know you and your competence by working with you.
3. Take on additional leadership roles in the community, like creating a meetup group in your area of expertise, organizing a conference, or becoming a mentor.
4. Assume thought leadership in topics you are passionate about and express your opinions by writing for newspapers or publishing a book.
5. Find ways to engage your network as you are building it by inviting them to events, showing up to events where they are present, and sharing valuable insights or information with them.

Self-Promoting vs. Branding

Branding is not the same as self-promotion. Self-promotion is when you are only talking about yourself and your achievements. If the purpose of your content is just to toot your own horn, stop. Your true purpose needs to be meaningful to others. As an example, my purpose is to open people's minds and hearts to new ways of thinking so that together we can create a society that is inclusive and enlightened. I do that by bringing to the surface ideas, beliefs, and challenges that are not always apparent, and I pose questions that challenge people to view things differently.

A colleague advised me once to not focus on my next career move but instead to focus on doing good work; it is usually rewarded. Unfortunately, that is what women have been told for decades: keep your head down, do good work, and you will be recognized and rewarded. In reality, this isn't what happens. If you don't work to promote yourself or make yourself visible or "seen," then you're relying on luck to create your future for you.

We not only have to do good work, but we have to ensure that we are getting credit for it. We have to be known as someone competent who people want to include on their teams. You do not have to play mediocre to make other people feel good. You owe it to the world to be recognized for your accomplishments and your potential.

Dos and Don'ts for Building Your Brand

<u>Do Not</u> Wave Your Medals Around at Every Opportunity.

Learn to articulate your achievements at the appropriate time in a tactful manner. Ask yourself when you should be talking about your accomplishments. If you are at a networking event and your intention is to find a new job, then yes, absolutely, promote yourself to a certain degree so that you are perceived as someone who can add value and contribute to a business. If, however, you are looking to get new customers, do not talk about yourself first; talk about your products and services, and supplement those details with remarks about who you are and why you are a trustworthy, qualified person who your potential customers would want to buy from.

Find an appropriate way to show your knowledge and competence—and the best way to do that is by adding value to other people's conversations. Instead of steering the conversation toward yourself, listen to what others are saying and add your wisdom and knowledge. People will notice you when you show that you notice them. Ask thoughtful, intelligent questions that subtly reveal your skills and competence.

<u>Do Not</u> Make Self-Aggrandizing Claims.

Avoid claims like "I am the best salesperson on my team" or humblebragging statements like "Oh, so annoying, my CEO wants me to present to the board next week in Paris. I am tired of traveling!" Instead, be genuine. Show that you are really excited to have been invited to present to the board again because your last presentation really helped them look at the problem through a different lens.

Do Put Yourself in Situations Where You Will Be Noticed.

Volunteer to present during the department and company meetings, or sign up as a speaker for a conference. If you were the analyst on a big project, ask your PM if you can present the results as part of the final delivery. Build relationships with mentors and supporters who can brag on your behalf.

Do Have an Elevator Pitch Ready.

Prepare a precise statement of who you are and what you do in advance of any big meetings or opportunities. That way, you always appear confident when you introduce yourself, and you avoid being unclear and going in circles. Make a good first impression with your eloquence.

Do Not Make Your Content All About You.

Make it about providing real value to your audience, and make it much more about others than yourself. It is okay to share your story if it is adding value to other people's lives and helps broaden their perspective. People crave authentic content, so don't be shy.

Do Reframe Talking about Yourself as Personal Branding.

Personal branding will help you achieve your future goals and add value to society and to business. It is not about you; it is about the impact that you want to create in the world.

We allow ourselves to be defined by the big corporate brands we work for, and to think that that is enough. It is not enough. Build a personal brand that stands on its own so you can create bigger impact, make more money, and get to work on more exciting projects sooner rather than later.

Remember, your brand does not have to be eternal. You can pivot your brand just as easily as you can pivot your career. As I moved away from corporate leadership to venture capital and investing, I further built on the brand that I had already built in the energy and maritime industry. Doors opened for me based on my existing brand, and I was given opportunities to invest in exclusive companies, all because of my brand. People wanted me on their cap tables, not only for the value I provided, but also for my brand name.

Once I became intentional about building my brand, the world of opportunities opened for me, I got promoted faster, got a seat at the board table, and made more money. You can do the same!

Chapter 15:

Building Resilience

The future rewards those who press on. I don't have time to feel sorry for myself. I don't have time to complain. I'm going to press on.

— *Barack Obama*

Resilience is our ability to stand in the face of a storm. Falling and stumbling against the opposing forces, but finding the strength to stand up again and keep going. Scarred, but strong and valiant.

Being resilient does not mean that you are unfazed, unmoved, and detached from what is going on. It is simply remaining in the storm, feeling it all, yet deciding—choosing—to get back up again. It is our ability to recover from setbacks quickly and start looking ahead.

Resilience is core to agile leadership built on the agile value "responding to change over following a plan." For leaders, resilience is about being able to lead your team through turmoil, chaos, and confusion. Furthermore, it is about how you have faith in yourself to come up with a new plan when things do not work out. It is about having a relentless focus on learning and improving to get to your goal.

Ask any successful person about their career journey, and they will tell you that it has been on the back of many setbacks and failures. If you are to achieve big things, you must take risks, and the more risks you take, the more you will be exposed to failure and success. Once I accepted that failure is a natural part of my career trajectory, I was able to reframe it as learning, as a stepping stone. Failure does not have to stop me from achieving my goals. It is a reminder for me to reflect on my journey, to assess if I am still on the desired path or if I need to pivot. A failure can be a launchpad that brings you closer to your next dream destination.

Ghosting

A few years ago, I applied for a new role at my company. I had three rounds of interviews, and we had a really good thing going. The hiring manager and his boss made it clear that I was perfect for the role.

And then I did not hear back.

I followed up with emails—no response. We worked in the same office building, so I went down to ask what was going on. They said that it was just taking longer than expected and assured me that I would be getting an offer.

Three months later, I got an automated email that said that the position had been filled. No one called to let me know. Again, I worked for the same company, in the same office building. I was sure to run into them.

I had been ghosted.

I had been in long conversations with them and had been beginning to build a relationship, when they just went completely silent. I was in a limbo, wondering if I should follow up directly or just let it go.

Ghosting is the new form of rejection in the digital era. People are opting out of awkward situations and difficult conversations in a world where we are more connected than ever before, not realizing the harmful impact of their complete disengagement on the workplace culture. For someone early on in their career, being ghosted can be a big blow to their confidence. Yet we cannot make people stop ghosting, and instead, we have to learn to build our resilience against all forms of rejection.

Processing Rejection

Rejections absolutely bring me down, especially if I am caught off guard and I am not expecting to be rejected—like another time, when I was again sure that I was going to get a certain job, I told everyone about it and started to plan and envision my life with the new job, and then suddenly, out of the blue, I got a rejection. For a short moment, my entire reality needed to readjust as I absorbed the shock. My mind and body needed time to accept the new reality. That can take a day or two or more, depending on how drastically different the new reality is. The more rejections I face, the more quickly I can get back on my feet, and the more resilient I become.

Resilience is not letting the pain of rejection hold us back from availing the next opportunity to succeed. I am optimistic by nature. Positivity is a strong value of mine. I love dreaming about the best-case scenario and giving it a real fighting chance. This means facing up to a lot of rejection. If I let every rejection eat at my ego, there won't be any ego left. In face of rejection, I tell myself to not take myself too seriously. When I adopt such an attitude, I stop feeding the ego. I look for humor in the situation; I look for the story I will tell ten years down the line about the rejection. In the grand scheme of things, one rejection says nothing about me and where I will go.

Acceptance

The first step to building resilience is accepting the circumstances you are in.

When HR called to let me know that, six months into my tenure in my new role, they were going to remove me and give me a new role, I was devastated because my biggest fear had manifested. Yet I was prepared. Subconsciously, my body had known what was coming. I had had a clear warning. Two months before, my boss, Mario, had given me some tough feedback, followed by the strange one-on-one meeting that became a three-on-three ambush that I described in chapter 1, where suddenly HR and my boss's boss had also appeared and grilled me on my performance.

For two months, I worked in panic mode. I was living in fear that I could lose my job at any moment. I was trying to do everything to make my boss happy, but I was losing myself in the process. After a few weeks of trying to do more work to make my manager happy and trying to be available to my team to be the leader that I really wanted to be, I realized that I could not. I could not operate at my highest level when I was being driven by fear. I was doing everything to try to hold on to the position, the title, the team, the stature.

I began to question myself. Why was I holding on to this role so tightly? What would letting go look like? What if this was not the end of the world? What if, instead of viewing the loss like a blow to my career, I let it be the best thing that ever happened to me?

Through these questions, I was beginning to accept that the way my boss wanted me to show up as a leader was not something I could give him. That did not make me weak; it did not make me inadequate or flawed. It did not mean that I could not do the job. It only meant that I could not do the job *the way he wanted me to do it*. I was beginning to face the facts and untangle my self-worth from my boss's feedback. His feedback was not about me; it was about him. It was about how he would have led in my position.

I was beginning to face the fear. Instead of holding on and trying to control everything, I decided to lean into the femininity within me. What if I became more fluid, more flexible, more like a river than a rock? When I am a rock, I am resisting change, I am trying to cling to a role that is meant to transform the organization when I myself am not willing to let the experience transform me. When I let myself become the river, I can flow with the pull of gravity, I can find a path around, over, under, and through the rocks to get to my destiny. Being a river allows me to continue growing, to continue exploring while surrendering to forces beyond me. Staying rock-solid, I will slowly erode due to the pressures surrounding me. Yet a river, in its very resilient nature, will spring back after a drought, open to changing, renewing, and moving forward.

I decided to tap into the adventurer within me and open up to the possibilities that this change could bring for me.

I reminded myself of my own words: "Leadership is not given, it is assumed." I do not need someone to give me a title or a promotion. The leader resides inside me. I had known this all along, but my ego was getting in my way, still seeking outside validation.

I was beginning to accept that change was imminent and it was not the end of the world. In fact, it was a new beginning. I just needed to be the river and trust myself.

Reframe

As you accept the circumstances, you can also begin to reframe the story.

I began to reframe what HR was telling me about my role. It was not a rejection; it was an opportunity. Ever since the feedback session with my boss, I had been on edge. I could feel the job slipping away from me. I was in a tug-of-war, wanting to do more so I could keep the job, but also wanting to lead in a way that felt true to me. Now the decision was made. I could finally stop trying to make it all work. I could let go.

At some level, I had started reframing the story even before that call from HR. As devastated as I was, I was ready; the news was not a shock. I had built resilience. I had decided to become water. I was ready to flow with the circumstances handed to me.

The words we use are important in how we see the world. *Rejection*, for example, is a loaded word. Reframe it as *redirection*, a *pivot*, or, better yet, *guidance* toward something better and bigger. Reframe events and scenarios into stories that are more empowering. A no from that one job you really wanted is simply more clarity on your next step; you can cross off that opportunity and focus on the next one you might not have even considered but that is even bigger. Closing one door is an opportunity to knock on others. It is very easy for the brain to turn to worst-case scenarios, but I try to think of the *best-case* scenario instead. What if losing one opportunity means that there is an even better opportunity waiting for me to find it? Without receiving a no, you would not know to look for and cast a broader net for opportunities.

How could I make losing what I had thought was my dream job into the best thing that had ever happened to me? Well, simply by creating even more exciting opportunities—thinking even bigger! What if losing my "dream job" was exactly what I needed at that time in my career, in order to really step it up a notch? What if it was an opportunity to jump out of the rat race and reinvent my career? What if it meant that I could finally focus on writing the book I had been wanting to write for more than a year? What if it meant that I could finally launch my podcast and start my own business? Wow—thinking about the endless possibilities really got me pumped up!

Take Action toward Your Desired Future

When you are in the valley of despair, recovering from a blow to your ego and your heart, the best thing you can do is take action. Phil Stutz, a leading psychiatrist, says in his Netflix documentary, "True confidence is living in uncertainty and still moving forward. The winner is the one who keeps moving, who takes the risk, is willing to act with some degree of faith, and then eats the consequences." He uses a metaphor of putting pearls on a string, where each pearl is an action and each action is given the same weight as the others. No matter how big or small each action may seem, how uncertain, your job is simply to keep adding more.[33]

Simply taking action, any action, small or big, helps you feel better. It prevents you from staying stuck, and, ultimately, it builds your resilience.

When I reframe a setback as a challenge or an opportunity, I can get really excited. I start looking forward. Even if I have not completely processed the loss, action makes me feel better. It puts me in a higher energy state.

After I got the news from HR, I was on my feet, ready for the next thing. I was done crying and feeling sorry for myself. It was time for me to put the armor back on and keep on chasing my dreams, to look ahead and find new opportunities.

The adrenaline kicked in, and I was on fire. I was ready to forget that this had ever happened and to move on. *This isn't my first rodeo. I have been defeated before. The pain is temporary. I am resilient.*

I got into action mode quickly, and, in retrospect, fighting and getting busy were easier than facing the pain under the armor. But pain takes time to process. I am still processing the pain, but moving forward helps tremendously as I begin to pick up my confidence and believe in myself again.

---

33   *Stutz,* directed by Jonah Hill, Netflix, 2022.

In the face of challenges, I make it a goal to act on even the most outrageous ideas immediately, as soon as the idea appears. When the first idea does not work out, I remind myself that it was just the first idea that came to my mind. It is time to brainstorm some more!

Ditch the Victim Mindset

There are many systematic biases that put women and people of color at a disadvantage in the workplace, and I covered many of those in chapter 4. We cannot take responsibility for everything, but we can choose to be empowered and to stay away from the victim mindset. We adopt the victim mindset when we believe that we have no control over things that happen to us and that everything and everyone is working against us. We ruminate and whip up stories in our heads about the injustices that have been done to us. Everyone is susceptible to the victim mindset, particularly in the face of setbacks.

Recognize when you are in that mode. I definitely felt myself falling into the whirlpool of such thoughts when I lost my job. The first step is to recognize and accept that you are falling into that mindset. The second step is to begin to shift your thoughts from being a victim to being a survivor (reframing). You are strong and can do hard things.

Ditching the victim mindset allows us to stop taking everything so personally and to believe that we have more control over our lives. As survivors, we adopt a mindset that we are the leaders of our lives and our careers. We can take responsibility for the good, the bad, and the ugly. We can take charge and dispel the limiting beliefs that are making us feel like victims.

Ask how you can be empowered and see a setback as an opportunity for change. In those weeks of despair, I told myself that I was the messenger, going through the experience so that I could truly understand a challenge that many feel. How could I use my platform to tell their stories by telling my own story?

Remember, you are not alone. Many great leaders have faced adversity. Take Sallie Krawcheck, the CEO of Ellevest and former banking executive whose rebellion expelled her from Wall Street but who went on to start a new financial model that served women. She was fired publicly twice, first from her job at Citigroup's wealth-management business and second from her job as president of her division at Bank of America. Her power was in reframing her expulsions as an opportunity to think different.

When I faced my own loss, I asked myself, "How can I take the journey that Santiago did in *The Alchemist* by Paulo Coelho?" Santiago gave all his money to a young boy to buy two camels, but the boy ran away with all his money. At that moment, Santiago could decide to think of himself as a poor victim of a thief or an adventurer in quest of his treasure. He chose to be an adventurer—and so did I. Yes, I may have lost my dream job, but that has allowed me to be an adventurer in search of my treasure, my true purpose. My loss was an opportunity to create a new dream.

Devise Systems That Allow You to Bounce Back

When I look back at my corporate career, I have been rejected, disappointed, and ended up in tears in many situations, but I do not regret taking the risks that I took; I regret not taking even bigger risks. The lows get blunted over time, but the accomplishments and the joy just pile up. The first blow hurts, but you develop a thicker skin. You have been through the struggle before, and your body and mind develop ways to overcome failure quicker.

Along with acceptance, reframing, taking action, and ditching the victim mindset, you can devise systems that allow you to bounce back up.

Here are ways that I am able to bounce back again:

1. Focus on the little things in life that bring you joy. My go-to remedies include going for a run, writing in my journal, confiding in a close friend, and hugging my kids to fill up my love cup. Figure out what the little things in life that bring you joy are and use them when going through an ordeal. Take a small step that can make you feel better, even if it's just a little bit better. Sometimes, these things may have minimal effect, and sometimes, they may make you feel infinitely better. Even small improvements in mood can accumulate to ease the pain and help you heal.

2. Establish uplifting daily routines. I love having a morning routine. Mine includes twenty minutes of yoga, reading, and writing in my journal for an hour before my kids get up. I do these things regardless of how I am feeling. These rituals are helpful when I have a bad day or a major setback at work. They help me reflect on who I am and who I am becoming. They help me recenter and see the world with more love and compassion.
    (Remember to get free access to my favorite daily journaling prompts to start journaling today at www. nadahmed.com/resources)

3. Build deeper connections with friends and mentors. Use this moment when you are not at your best to connect with someone. Being vulnerable allows us to make deeper connections. Reach out for help. Many people worry that reaching out to others with their problems is a burden, but in fact, in most situations, your mentors and friends will be grateful. That is what they are there for. Research shows that helping others is the most efficient healing strategy, so you could even try to reach out to someone who needs you, and you may find ways to help each other.

I felt so many different emotions when I lost my role: disappointment, shame, regret, anger, resentment. Through all of it, I stuck to the systems I had devised. I went running even more consistently, even if, at times, I had to stop mid-run because I found myself sobbing profusely. I let out the emotions and kept going. Knowing that I had still managed to get my run in on hard days made me feel resilient. It built my confidence. During this period, I established an even more stringent morning routine, where I got up at 4:30 a.m. to meditate, journal, and read uplifting books. This allowed me to go deeper within myself and process the shame that came with the loss. I used my community of friends and mentors extensively. I really do not know what I would have done without my coach, my mentor, and my mastermind friends. By being vulnerable, I built stronger connections with them. I allowed them into my pain so they could help me.

I recognized that, during this time, I needed self-love. I found joy in lighting candles every morning when I woke up before dusk. I was awake and in a positive state of mind to receive my kids when they woke up and came running out of the living room to find me meditating or doing yoga. I embraced them with all my soul and enjoyed the precious morning moments with them. We made breakfast and cuddled a lot. The systems you put in place become the foundation on which you can stay grounded and be ready to bounce back.

You will also go through your own cycles of grief in your career, when dreams are interrupted, relationships are cut off, and hopes are squandered. You will fall apart, only so that you can be put back together even stronger, with more empathy, compassion, and a stronger sense of purpose. Build systems now so that when you are struck, you have something to fall on. Find a community of mentors, colleagues, and friends who will cheer you on, regardless of success or failure. Build these connections now so that you can reach out to them when you are feeling vulnerable. Build a daily routine that allows you to take regular action toward something you care about, even if the action is small. These routines will help get your through the low points of your career journey so you can reach that peak again.

Resilience is something that you work on every single day to keep negative stories about yourself and others at bay. Find meaning in adversity, be optimistic, take action, and accept that change is part of life and part of a successful career.

Chapter 16:

Embracing All of Me

Your time is limited, so don't waste it living someone else's life. Don't be trapped by dogma—which is living with the results of other people's thinking. Don't let the noise of others' opinions drown out your own inner voice. And most important, have the courage to follow your heart and intuition.'

— *Steve Jobs*

"Nada, I am new to the company and this role. I do not know you yet. You have to prove yourself to me."

Famous last words from my new boss. I had decided to go along with the restructuring and accepted the new role proposed to me by HR. I needed time to process the loss and all the other feelings that came with it. However, these words from my new boss were the straw that broke the camel's back.

Prove myself?

Her words hit me with an epiphany like a lightning bolt. Tiny fireworks went off in my brain. It was as if she knew exactly what I needed to hear at that moment, as if she had pulled out a mirror so that I could see a true reflection of myself.

I had lived all my life trying to prove myself. I had wanted to show everyone who did not believe in me that I could win, that I had the grit and the stamina. I had wanted to prove to all the naysayers that I was worth taking seriously. But when would it be enough? Who says, "Stop, now you have proven yourself"?

My boss's words were a gift. They peeled off another layer of the mask that I was hiding behind, the mask of trying to prove myself to others and to myself. My boss's words gave me the realization that I did not need this mask anymore.

This was my moment of awakening. I had proven myself. I had made it. I had done the work, assumed leadership, gotten the medals, done and said the right things, and achieved everything on my list and more.

This realization was so liberating that I decided to hand in my resignation after having just accepted the new role. I no longer needed to stay, as I was no longer working to prove myself to others. I no longer needed that validation, that rubber stamp of approval from corporate.

I did not know what I was going to do next. But I trusted myself to figure it out.

You will also reach that defining point in your career when you ask yourself, "What am I chasing? Who am I doing this for? What am I running away from?" The thoughts will appear unexpectedly and take you by surprise. Losing my dream job was the catalyst for me, a gift in ugly wrapping, a way out. It brought me to my hour of awakening, a request to go within myself to understand what I really wanted.

I was thrust out of orbit, so I could look at the universe around me and realize that I had options, that I could go in any direction that I wanted. I had been circling around this one planet that I had imagined to be the center of the universe, my true desire, my raison d'être, when in fact, I could choose. I could choose to be whatever I wanted to be, wherever I wanted to be.

I had to have the experiences I had had, the good, the bad, and the ugly, to arrive where I was, to be the person who would be able to see the possibilities of the endless universe.

The person who could walk away from adversity with her self-worth, her self-confidence, and her ambitions intact. The person who could see that going back to another high-flying role at another company was not going to solve the problem. To step up, I needed to step aside and out of orbit. I had to confront my inner demons because whatever I was fighting and running away from was not outside me, but within me.

I am wrapped up in an identity of a woman, a woman representing all of womankind, who is in eternal rebellion, fighting for equality and justice. A woman who is a bit on the edge, always on the lookout for injustice, bias, and discrimination. In search of freedom, I do not want to become a slave to my own rebellion. When you look for problems, they will find you. When you look for opportunity, opportunities are all you see. Should I continue to scrutinize the system and look for problems, or should I embrace the opportunities at every corner?

I was ready to let go of the twelve-year-old rebel inside, to set her free, to let her fly. She was ready to explore the skies, beyond what was currently in sight, into the greater unknown, a vast new reality.

As Albert Camus is believed to have once said, "The only way to deal with an unfree world is to become so absolutely free that your very existence is an act of rebellion."

Now that I was free, how could I affect change from a place of freedom, from a place of love and compassion for everybody?

That is the next chapter of my life.

You always have options when dreams crumble. You can curl up in your bed and wallow in despair, or you can fire up the rebel inside. Take the time to recover, but then fuel the part of you that is determined to lead, determined to chart an alternate path, that still believes in the dream even if that dream seems to be eviscerated at the moment.

I want you to rebel and drive change, but don't become a slave to it. Don't go down the negative downward spiral of victimhood. Realize that you have more control over your life than you think.

Challenge the status quo from a place of love. Let go of anger and resentment. It does not serve you. Let go to set yourself free.

And when you are free, your very existence becomes an act of rebellion.

Conclusion

You are a child of God. Your playing small does not serve the world. There is nothing enlightened about shrinking so that other people won't feel insecure around you. We are all meant to shine, as children do. We were born to make manifest the glory of God that is within us. It's not just in some of us; it's in everyone. And as we let our own light shine, we unconsciously give other people permission to do the same. As we are liberated from our own fear, our presence automatically liberates others.

— *Marianne Williamson*

You are not alone on this journey. I share your dreams and aspirations, and I am cheering you on every step of the way. My hope is that, with this book, I provide you with what you need to transform your career and set yourself free.

I want you to know that anyone who truly desires to lead can become a leader. There will be barriers, there will be setbacks, and there will be disappointments, all serving a purpose: to transform you into the leader you are becoming, the leader you desire to be. Everything is strategically put in place to reveal to you how you will lead and why you will lead.

It is okay to get impatient and frustrated when progress is slow. In those moments, take a look back at how much ground you have covered. Sometimes, incremental progress is hard to see. You might just be at the precipice of your big quantum leap. Don't lose hope now; just be ready.

Be ready with your stellar self-confidence, your rock-solid faith that you have come this far and can go a lot further. Do not let any doubts settle in your head about your ability, your ambitions, and your value. Yes, there will be challenges. We all face them. Take them in stride. They are nothing personal; they have nothing to do with your grit and your ability. You are growing, and growth can be painful. Stay open to allyship and support so that you do not go through the uncomfortable parts of the journey alone.

As leaders, our work is to show that everyone will benefit from a diverse of way of working, being, and thinking. We belong here. To drive change, we have to be part of the system. We have to be part of redesigning the workplace for ourselves, for all of us who are different and unique.

Let's continue to show up with a wide variety of leadership attributes. Let's be vulnerable, collaborative, kind, strong, assertive, creative, structured, and analytical. Let's not close up our feelings; let's not disconnect our hearts. Vulnerability allows us to connect with people, and connection allows us to be better leaders.

In this new women's movement, let's embrace our femininity. Let's not be afraid to show our feminine sides and bring them to the table. Let's shine light on the female values that are beneficial for business. Let's be part of creating a new system that is more inclusive, open, and accepting.

The generation of women who came before us fought for our basic rights. Suffragists started a movement that gave us the freedom we have today. Let's work with the men and women of today to ensure that not only do we as a gender thrive in business and have successful careers, but we can be ourselves completely. Instead of leaving our femininity behind, let's find meaning in it. It is our strength; it is our superpower. Equality in the workplace is not about being treated exactly the same. It is about equity, that we recognize our differences, not only as men and women, but as individuals, so we can devise ways to leverage those differences to produce our best work.

When you start uprooting deeply held beliefs that hold you back, you will begin to build a career that is meaningful and deeply fulfilling to you. You will stop doubting yourself and truly start believing in your abilities. You will find purpose, and it will become much harder to hold yourself back.

When you have clarity on who you want to become and what skills you want to hone and you stop caring about what other people think, you will start raising your hand and will begin to show up with courage. When you show up with courage, confidence follows, and the world will move in magical ways to start presenting you with opportunities.

Assert your boundaries. That is your right. Boundaries are protections that are necessary for us to continue with our mission with love and compassion for others and for ourselves.

As agile leaders, our job is to make space for everyone to speak up, voice their concerns, and feel included and comfortable. Our job is collaboration. It is through collaboration that we come up with breakthrough solutions and are able to execute them effectively. A collaborative environment is more fun for everyone involved, so focus on creating high-performance teams instead of high-performance individuals.

Freedom is letting go of trying to change other people, but rather focusing on being unapologetically yourself. You are the change. You are the hero of the story, and you will continue to play a pivotal role in your movie. In those weeks of despair when I lost my dream job, I kept on asking myself, "Why is this happening *for* me? How can this experience expand my horizons and give me more depth so I can go even further with my ambitions?"

Don't let your ambition be rooted in unhealthy insecurities about trying to prove yourself to others who have done you wrong, or even in proving yourself to the little girl inside of you. If you are reading this book, chances are that you have already covered significant distance in your life. You have faced hard things and you have developed unique skills that others will envy. Live as if you have proven yourself.

I hope this book gives you tools that you can take with you on your journey, some way of taking bold action toward your ambitions today. Get curious about your unique abilities, build your confidence in them, and use the tools you have at hand today to build a brand around your competence and expertise that will last way into the future. Stay determined. Take the reins; be your own voice; be your own amplifier.

If freedom is what we are going for, let's create that freedom today, for freedom is in the mind and the heart.

Next Steps

Thank you for coming with me on this journey. If you enjoyed this book, do let me know by getting in touch (support@nadahmed.com or LinkedIn) and by leaving the book a review on Amazon.

You can sign up to my newsletter to receive leadership tips and stay posted on events, webinars, podcasts, and courses relevant to you: www.nadahmed.com/resources.

If you feel inspired and wish to follow me further, here are my social media contacts:

- LinkedIn:https://www.linkedin.com/in/nadaahmed-agileleadership/
- Instagram, Twitter, and TikTok: @thisisnadaahmed

Feel free to get in touch to book me for speaking gigs, podcasts, leadership training, and advisory work. You can email support@nadahmed.com or connect through my website, www.nadahmed.com.

I launch two masterminds a year, one for women in leadership and the other for women in venture capital. Find more information on my website: www.nadahmed.com/mastermind

Check out my podcasts:

- **Braving Innovation:** A podcast on leadership, innovation, and entrepreneurship
- **Women Writing Checks:** A podcast for women in venture capital

Both are available on Apple Podcasts, Google Podcasts, and Spotify.

Acknowledgments

This book would not have been possible without the unwavering support of friends, family, and leadership mentors. I would like to thank my mother for always inspiring me, for listening to me talk for hours about my book and my aspirations for myself and my career, and for providing valuable advice and words of wisdom along the way. I would also like to thank my sister, Ozen, for being a role model mother and successful banker in a highly male-dominated space and my brother, Hassan, for being the rational voice of reason and my dad for his unwavering support.

Thank you to my husband for tolerating my very early morning routines to write this book and for always being available to brainstorm ideas for the book and what direction it may be taking. Thank you to my two kids, Kian and Kaira, who are the source of constant light and happiness in my life and have taught me to be present and happy in the moment. In fact, my most important lessons on leadership come from my kids!

Thank you, Rita Hausken, my leadership coach, who has literally held my hand through some of the most transformational moments in my career and been the pillar of support that allowed me to continue believing in myself and my dreams. Your wisdom, your depth, and your empathy are beyond measure.

Thank you to my mentor, Liv Monica Stubholt, who has been on this journey with me since the very beginning. I have no idea where I would be without her wisdom and advice. She has been my savior, my constant support, my cheerleader, and my dear friend. She is with me to celebrate each one of my career milestones, and she provides me with the clarity I need to move on.

Thank you to my friend Kristine (Grecuhina) Kjos for understanding me, for cheering me on my journey, and for being an amazing role model, friend, and that disruptive woman who is determined to lead.

Thank you to my superwoman editor, Yna Davis, who went above and beyond to make this the best editing process, giving me detailed guidance every step of the way so I never felt lost or alone. Your advice and tips have meant so much to me.

Last but not least, thank you to my book coach, Jake Kelfer, for pushing me and inspiring me to keep on going. This book would not have been possible without your guidance and constant support.

About the Author

Nada Ahmed is a corporate leader turned entrepreneur, strategy and innovation expert, board member, and angel investor. She has over fifteen years of global corporate leadership and innovation experience within the energy, climate tech, and maritime industries. She is a world-renowned speaker and writer on the topics of leadership, innovation, and diversity and inclusion.

Through her company, Agile Leadership, Nada helps customers catapult revenue and gain a competitive advantage through innovation, ruthless prioritization, and robust go-to-market strategies. She serves as an advisor to many startups and sits on the board of small and medium-sized companies where innovation and growth are top priorities. She is also active within the venture capital community, supporting and investing in startups.

Nada is a true global citizen, having lived in Pakistan, the United States, France, Norway, and Hong Kong. Nada was on the 2020 list of the top fifty women in technology awarded by Abelia and ODA-Network in Norway and was on the 2021 list of high-achieving leaders under forty awarded by the Foreign Ministry of Pakistan.

Nada is the host of two podcasts, B*raving Innovation*, a podcast about innovation and leadership, and *Women Writing Checks*, a podcast for women in venture capital. The podcasts bring inspiring stories, tips, and strategies from leaders all around the world to help entrepreneurs, innovation leaders, and investors succeed in their journeys. Tune in for LinkedIn Live sessions every week or search *Braving Innovation* or *Women Writing* Checks on Spotify and Apple Podcasts, or go to https://nadahmed.podbean.com/ to listen.

Leave This Book a Review

Dear fellow leaders,

If you liked this book, I would love it if you would leave me a review so that I can reach more people with this book and impact more lives.

Thank you!

Bibliography

"2022 State of the Gender Pay Gap Report." Payscale. March 15, 2022. https://www. payscale.com/research-and-insights/gender-pay-gap/.

"Biote Women in the Workplace Survey." Biote. Last updated May 10, 2022 https:// biote.com/learning-center/biote-women-in-the-workplace-survey.

"Report of the Task Group on Reference Man." *Annals of the ICRP* 3, no. 1–4 (1975): iii. https://doi.org/10.1016/0146-6453(79)90123-4.

"The Double-Bind Dilemma for Women in Leadership: Damned If You Do, Doomed If You Don't (Report)." Catalyst. July 15, 2007. https://www.catalyst.org/ research/the-double-bind-dilemma-for-women-in-leadership-damned-if-you-do-doomed-if-you-dont/.

"The monk and the empty boat." A Feeling of Symmetry. November 28, 2020. https://afeelingofsymmetry.com/the-monk-and-the-empty-boat/. Adapted from Hạnh, Thích Nhất. *Being Peace.* Berkeley: Parallax Press, 1987.

Ahmed, Nada. "E17: Dr. Mara Harvey on Financial Literacy, Taking Control of Our Finances and What We Can Teach Our Kids." *Braving Innovation.* September 11, 2022. Podcast, MP3 audio, 37:37. https://nadahmed.podbean.com/e/e16-dr-mara-harvey-on-financial-literacy-taking-control-of-our-finances-and-what-we-can-teach-our-kids/.

Ananthaswamy, Anil and Kate Douglas. "How Protective Parents Exacerbate Gender Differences." *New Scientist.* April 18, 2018. https://www.newscientist. com/article/mg23831740-700-how-protective-parents-exacerbate-gender-differences/.

Beedle, Mike et al. "Manifesto for Agile Software Development." Accessed January 23, 2023. https://agilemanifesto.org/.

Boorstin, Julia Boorstin. *When Women Lead: What They Achieve, Why They Succeed, and How We Can Learn from Them.* Avid Reader Press, 2022.

Boorstin, Julia. "The Most Successful Women CEOs Lead Differently. Here's What We Can Learn from Them." LinkedIn. October 13, 2022. https://www.linkedin. com/pulse/most-successful-women-ceos-lead-differently-heres-what-julia-boorstin/.

Brown, Brené. "Brené with James Clear on *Atomic Habits*, Part 1 of 2." *Dare to Lead with Brené Brown.* November 15, 2021. Podcast, 49:51. https://brenebrown.com/podcast/atomic-habits-part-1-of-2/.

Edmondson, Amy C. *The Fearless Organization: Creating Psychological Safety in the Workplace for Learning, Innovation, and Growth.* Hoboken, NJ: John Wiley & Sons, 2018.

Goldman, Bruce. "Two Minds: The Cognitive Differences between Men and Women." *Stanford Medicine Magazine.* Spring 2017. https://stanmed.stanford.edu/how-mens-and-womens-brains-are-different/.

Green, Paul. "Shopping for Confirmation: How Disconfirming Feedback Shapes Social Networks." Harvard Business School Working Paper No. 18-028. September 20, 2017. http://dx.doi.org/10.2139/ssrn.3040066.

Hamel, Gary and Michele Zanini. *Humanocracy: Creating Organizations as Amazing as the People Inside Them.* Boston: Harvard Business Review Press, 2020.

Hill, Amelia. "More than 1m UK Women Could Quit Their Jobs through Lack of Menopause Support." *The Guardian.* January 17, 2022. https://www.theguardian.com/society/2022/jan/17/more-than-1m-uk-women-could-quit-their-jobs-through-lack-of-menopause-support.

Hill, Jonah, dir. *Stutz.* 2022: Netflix.

King Jr., Martin Luther. *Strength to Love.* Minneapolis: Fortress Press, 1963.

Krawcheck, Sallie. "3 Pieces of Career Advice You Won't Hear Anywhere Else." Ellevest. August 9, 2022. https://www.ellevest.com/magazine/career/sallie-krawcheck-top-career-advice/.

Kray, Laura and Margaret Lee. "The Pay Gap for Women Starts with a Responsibility Gap." *Wall Street Journal.* October 14, 2021. https://www.wsj.com/articles/the-pay-gap-for-women-starts-with-a-responsibility-gap-11634224762.

Krivkovich, Alexis, Wei Wei Liu, Hilary Nguyen, Ishanaa Rambachan, Nicole Robinson, Monne Williams, and Lareina Yee. "Women in the Workplace 2022." McKinsey & Company. October 18, 2022. https://www.mckinsey.com/featured-insights/diversity-and-inclusion/women-in-the-workplace.

Langved, Åshild and Espen Linderud. "Kvinnene er lønnstapere i Oljefondet – og de får sjeldnere bonus" Dagens Næringsliv. March 7, 2018. https://www.dn.no/marked/norges-bank-investment-management/norges-bank/oljefondet/kvinnene-er-lonnstapere-i-oljefondet-og-de-far-sjeldnere-bonus/2-1-283576.

Mandela, Nelson. Long Walk to Freedom. Little, Brown and Company, 1994.

Perez, Caroline Criado. Invisible Women: Exposing Data Bias in a World Designed for Men. Broadway, NY: Abrams Press, 2019.

Roosevelt, Theodore. 1910. "Citizenship in a Republic." Transcript of speech delivered at the Sorbonne, Paris, France, April 23, 1910. https://www.presidency.ucsb.edu/documents/address-the-sorbonne-paris-france-citizenship-republic.

Sagmoen, Ingvild. "Bare 13 av de nesten 200 selskapene på Oslo Børs styres av kvinner: – Vi har ikke vært gode nok til å jobbe med å få frem kvinner." E24. Last updated June 23, 2019. https://e24.no/naeringsliv/i/9vxBod/bare-13-av-de-nesten-200-selskapene-paa-oslo-boers-styres-av-kvinner-vi-har-ikke-vaert-gode-nok-til-aa-jobbe-med-aa-faa-frem-kvinner.

Schulte, Brigid, Alieza Durana, Brian Stout, and Jonathan Moyer. "Paid Family Leave: How Much Time Is Enough?" New America. Last updated June 16, 2017. https://www.newamerica.org/better-life-lab/reports/paid-family-leave-how-much-time-enough/economic-impact/.

Steven Bartlett. "E184: World Leading Life Coach: 3 Steps To Figuring Out ANYTHING You Want: Marie Forleo." The Diary Of A CEO with Steven Bartlett. October 5, 2022. Podcast, MP3 audio, 1:33:49. https://podcasts.apple.com/gb/podcast/the-diary-of-a-ceo-with-steven-bartlett/id1291423644.

Tulshyan, Ruchika. "This question directed to Prime Ministers Jacinda Ardern (NZ) and Sanna Marin (Finland) was so offensive but a reminder of the daily aggressions women face." LinkedIn. Accessed January 24, 2023. https://www.linkedin.com/posts/rtulshyan_this-question-directed-to-prime-ministers-activity-7003760128684408832-UvXV/.

Ward, Marguerite. "Women Are Afraid to Call Themselves 'Ambitious' at Work and It's Seriously Hurting Their Careers." Insider. March 8, 2020. https://www.businessinsider.com/psychologist-recommend-strategies-ambition-women-at-work-career-goals.

Made in the USA
Middletown, DE
26 February 2023

25381991R00144